58 Feet

58 Feet
The Second That Changed Our Lives
By Mark and Robyn Glaser

Glaser, Mark and Robyn, Authors
58 Feet: The Second That Changed Our Lives

ISBN 978-1492149651

1. Memoir, 2. Family, 3. Health & Fitness: Physical Impairments

58 Feet

The Second
that Changed
Our Lives

Mark & Robyn Glaser

Dedication

This book is dedicated to my family
who never lost hope,
provided support and inspiration,
even when I didn't know it was being applied.

We are Craig!

NOBODY WAKES UP in the morning and believes that their lives will change in some unexpected instant ... a tragic event. When a traumatic event occurs, every community has a hospital or medical treatment available, but there is only one Craig.

Located in our backyard is a world-renowned, not-for-profit rehabilitation hospital called Craig Hospital, aka "Craig". Since 1956 Craig has graduated more than 29,000 people from all 50 states and multiple countries worldwide. Because of the 91% success rate in returning patients to their homes, work or school to live independent lives, Craig is ranked as a Top Ten Rehabilitation Hospital in the US.

Craig Hospital is a family of professionals that know how to care for people, support the families of their patients and help the injured "Redefine Possible." I suffered a traumatic brain injury (TBI) as a result of a motorcycle accident my wife and I were involved in, and with the help of the Craig Family, I was able to receive the treatment I needed to return to "normal." Craig Hospital was able to provide training, treatment, and most importantly, hope to our family in a time of real need; a service they provide happily to many who suffer from TBIs and spinal cord injuries.

We are Craig!

Introduction

K IDS, THIS IS a story about a life detour and the power and light of the human spirit.

Life is an adventure with many unpredictable changes along its path. As I've said, nobody ever wakes up in the morning and believes their life will change forever. And when the unimaginable happens, support from family, friends, colleagues and even complete strangers will help guide you back to where you want to be.

Our families have deep roots as ranchers, farmers, athletes, pilots, community leaders and business visionaries. You have wonderful family on both sides of the tree: Zedo (my dad – your grandpa), my mom Nancy (Grandma Nancy), your Uncle Chris and Aunt Nikki, along with their families. Your mom's parents – Gerald and Bonnie, and your Aunts: Brenda, Kristi, Dixie and Jenny, and their families. Each of them helped shape the foundation of who we are and who we will become, and the reason why your mother and I are married.

"I think about the years I've spent, just passing through
I'd like to have the time I lost, and give it back to you
But you just smile and take my hand
You've been there, you understand
It's all part of a grander plan
that is coming true"
"God Bless the Broken Road – By Rascal Flatts"
... our first dance song

The lyrics of this should always remind you of how your mother and I feel about each other, and how we want you to understand that time reveals your hidden treasures.

This is the story about how all of our lives were changed before you were even born. How each of our family members supported us during difficult times and have continued to care for both of you in ways that you will only understand as you grow and get to know each of them. This is also a story about the great extended family we have – friends, acquaintances and the Craig Hospital Family.

It takes a family to prop you up and support you, especially when you don't even know what you need.

We are so blessed to have so many caring people involved in our lives. These are the people who will help guide you thru the many challenges that you will face in life. Remember them, and remember to honor what they have done and will do.

Love – your mom and dad

A Note to Readers

This story is compiled from journal notes taken by many, posts to a Caring Bridge website, conversations with family, friends and medical staff, and personal experiences. Italicized entries are taken from posts on Caring Bridge by my sister-in-law, Robyn and Mark.

Early Morning, August 18, 2010

"CHRIS – CHRIS" . . . I say in a strained voice
"Yeah – are you ok? What do you need?"
"Can you get me a wet towel for my head?"

It's dark, the TV is on next to my bed with a Spanish infomercial on, I have a tube sticking through my nose and several wires hooked up to my chest and arm, but somehow I know where I am and what is happening . . .

My brother Chris is asleep in a chair at the end of my bed. I wake him somehow, and ask for a wet towel to put on my forehead. Chris gets the towel, puts it on my head and goes back to sleep.

This is my last night at St Anthony's and the first thing I really remember. There are other things that I can recall, I can remember happening, but I have no sense of when or why these events occurred.

The next day, I wake in a stretcher being pushed by two ambulance techs down the hall of the hospital. My wife Robyn and my father, whose name is David, but everyone calls Zedo—a Slavic word meaning grandfather—are walking behind, and Chris and Wes follow them. The ambulance workers keep talking to me about what is going on and asking if I know my name, where I am, what year it is . . . and then I fall back to sleep.

In the next moment, I am in an ambulance and being asked some of the same questions. Robyn is riding in the front seat of the ambulance and can't hear what was being said or asked. One of the techs is a younger gentleman who introduced himself as Rook. He said that he was a rookie, so the other guys called him Rook. His name was actually Ryan.

Ryan keeps asking me, "What is your name . . . when is your birthday . . . do you know where you are . . . do you know where you are going . . . do you know what happened?" He is making notes as I answer when I say, "Just take me home . . . I want to go home". Of course, Ryan can't let me leave.

I say that I don't want to go to the hospital and that I am feeling better.

Ryan explains again why we have to go to Craig Hospital and that it will be good for me.

I remain insistent on going home though. I tell Ryan, "I don't know how much you guys are being paid for today, but if you take me home, I have cash . . . I can pay you."

Ryan laughs and says that we still have to go to Craig. As he speaks, I fall back to sleep.

I wake up in a room at Craig, with Dr. Weintraub, who introduces himself as the primary physician on the team of professionals that are going to be working to help me with my injuries. He tells me that he is the concussion doctor for the Broncos and the Avalanche and will start his treatment evaluation immediately.

I ask Dr. Weintraub if he knows Dr. Anderson, my chiropractor . . .

Dr Weintraub says, "Yes I do . . . I don't think he'll be

cracking your back for a while though".

He starts asking me a bunch of questions:

"What is your name?"

"Mark Glaser."

"What year is it?"

"2010."

"Do you know where you are?"

"Craig Hospital."

"Do you know why you are here?"

"I was in a motorcycle accident."

"Do you know who the president is?"

"Barack Obama."

"Count backwards from 100 by 7's."

"93 – 86 – 79 . . . "

"Listen to me . . . I said count backwards from 100 by 7's."

"100 – 93 – 86 – 79 . . . "

"OK – now say the alphabet backwards."

"Z – Y – X – W – V – U . . . "

"OK – we treat our patients a little differently here. We don't use medication, so we will start taking you off all the medication that you were given at St Anthony's. You will start to feel the difference, but if you need something for the pain, just let us know."

I fall back to sleep. My best friend Stephen, who I've known since we met at work in1987, told me about the motorcycle accident sometime while I was awake, but not in a cognitive state at St Anthony's. Robyn and a Craig Hospital representative explained Craig Hospital to me, but I don't remember having that conversation.

Robyn and Zedo are meeting with the hospital patient/family coordinator. Melissa is a very nice young lady and explains the culture and environment at Craig Hospital.

Robyn really likes Melissa, and when we see her now, she is still so nice. It is made very clear to Robyn that things are going to be different at Craig. Now that I am at Craig, the medical staff will be focusing on my brain injury. Melissa explains that for the past four weeks, the intent of every treatment, doctor and procedure was simply to keep me alive . . . now I need to be taught how things are going to be different as a result of my brain injury. Melissa hands Robyn and Zedo a large three-ring binder detailing brain injuries, and helps them understand what to expect. In addition to being a great resource, Melissa is a wonderful person to be around and is very supportive.

People can tell from the first few moments at Craig that things are different . . . different in a comfortable way. Although this is a hospital, none of the medical staff wear scrubs . . . everyone smiles and is positive, and they go out of their way to help everyone.

Dr. Weintraub meets with Robyn and my father and tells them what to expect . . . I will be very tired, and the first week at Craig will be spent evaluating my injury and doing tests. I will be moving to and from therapy appointments, having X-Rays completed and getting a lot of rest. He tells Robyn and Zedo that I am not to have many visitors, and if there are any, the visitors have to keep their visits short, speak in a normal tone, speak slowly and try not to use complicated words.

Dr. Weintraub tells me that there will be nothing on our schedule for the first week, as I need to rest.

Next I meet the nurse and the speech therapist, Bert and Deb. I am informed that my schedule will be on the wall by the door and that I need to stay in bed. Of course, if I need anything, I can ask the nurse, who will be in the room around the clock for the first few days.

I share a room with another patient the first night, and have a nurse and technician with me all the time. Whenever I have to go to the bathroom, I have to ask the tech for help. When I move in bed, I need assistance. I am restricted to the use of a wheelchair because of the 45 pounds of weight I have lost and the associated loss of strength. I have to use a gait belt; a stabilizing belt designed to help move patients who struggle on their own, just to go to the restroom. In my own mind, of course, I still have all of the independence that I'd ever enjoyed, and remain hesitant to admit that I still need the help. This is very frustrating for me, as I have always prided myself on my physical conditioning and knowing my body. Right now I don't know who I am.

My physical therapist Stacey, comes in to introduce herself and explain what she is going to help with. She asks me to sit up in bed and swing my legs around to put my shoes on.

I hang my legs off the bed and ask for help.

Stacey: "Go ahead and put your shoes on"

"I can't."

"What do you mean you can't . . . you haven't even tried. Put your shoes on. Why do they always give me the big guys?"

Grrrr – I go ahead and lean over, and slip my shoes on. The experience is entirely unpleasant. My ribs still hurt and because of the neck collar, I can't move my head at all.

Stacey goes ahead and ties my shoes and puts the gait belt on me. She helps me out of bed and into a wheelchair. I tell Stacey that I don't need the chair and can walk . . . but Stacey was going to have none of that—she tells me to sit in the chair and she will ask the tech to take me where I want to go. When I try to move myself, I experience a sharp stabbing pain in my shoulder. I'm also suddenly aware of unexpected weakness in my arm. There's something wrong with my shoulder, but Stacey suggests that we could deal with it later. In the meantime, I should stop making excuses.

The day tech assigned to me is Carolyn and she is nice; always willing to help and likes to talk. The afternoon tech is Paul, and he is a great guy . . . a car fanatic; good for me to talk to. Robyn knows that I will like Paul.

I still have the trach in my throat so talking is difficult, and the yonker, a small tube that is attached to a suction machine and is inserted into the throat thru the trach, still has to be used frequently to clear my throat. I still have a feeding tube in my nose going to my stomach so I can get nutrients. Anytime that I want to get up or move in the wheelchair, the feeding tube, yonker and fluid bag have to be moved from the bedpost to the wheelchair IV post.

Between the brain injury, the neck surgery and my restricted diet, all I want to do is sleep. When I tell Robyn that I want some water, I learn that I am not allowed to have any yet. I tell her that I want to go home, but she has to explain to me that I can't yet. She asks me if there is anything from home that I would like. I tell Robyn, "no . . . I'm only going to be here for 2 weeks."

Zedo tells me, "You will probably be here longer than 2 weeks – don't push it. You need to rest and listen to the doctors."

It is only later when it becomes clear how serious my situation is and how lucky I was to be alive.

Over the following couple of days I start to piece together what happened during the last four weeks. The story starts on the back of a rental Harley and a magical weekend along State Highway 40 . . .

Friday, July 16th, 2010; one month earlier

MY WIFE ROBYN and I had been married for almost two years when we had this accident. We both like to travel, and have taken several weekend or day trips on "the hog," a 2001 Harley Softtail. Since summer was growing to a close, it was time to venture out again and enjoy some days on the road. The hog was nice, but it just wasn't comfortable for both of us to ride for long distances. I loved riding the motorcycle, and although Robyn didn't like it as much as I did, she would go on trips and try to have fun. But to enjoy these excursions more, we needed a motorcycle that was more comfortable for longer trips. So we began passively looking for another motorcycle and I suggested that we rent a touring bike while ours had to go to the shop for service.

On July 16th, I took the hog to the shop for service and rented a Harley Davidson Ultra-Glide. A very helpful representative from the shop, got us the bike we wanted to ride, convinced me to pay a little extra for the collision insurance and got us on our way.

We were on our way for an open weekend . . . no agenda – no specific path – just some time together!

So off we went . . . no real plan other than to travel the mountains, the open road, and enjoy time together. We left the house mid-morning and stopped in Golden for lunch. I thought it would be nice to travel towards Steamboat Springs, Grand Junction, Montrose, Colorado Springs and home. After leaving Golden, we drove over Berthoud pass, into Winter Park and continued towards Steamboat. Arriving into Steamboat late afternoon, we started looking for a hotel. Unbeknownst to us, a youth soccer tournament was being held in town that weekend and hotel rooms were scarce. Luckily, we finally found a room in an old hotel downtown that was perfect. It was across the street from a local BBQ restaurant, a favorite food of ours, where we had a fun meal and called it a day.

The next morning, we left Steamboat mid-morning and headed west towards Dinosaur, to turn south and into Grand Junction. Along the way, just outside of Dinosaur, we saw a couple of dogs walking along the side of the road.

Dog lovers that we are, we stopped to see if they were lost or hurt. Neither dog had a collar on, and it appeared that one of the dogs was older and was having some difficulty. Since we were on the motorcycle, there was certainly no room for two dogs, but we were able to at least share some of our water with them. When we arrived in Dinosaur, we went into the visitor's center and asked the staff if they could call the animal control department, and notify them of these lost or abandoned dogs. If we had been in our Tahoe, we would have been owners of 2 more dogs.

We continued south, and after lunch, the adventure continued on a route towards Grand Junction. Along the way, I noticed the bike blowing some oil. So when we got to town, I stopped to have the local Harley dealership take a look at the bike. The service was done quickly and efficiently, and the technicians had us on the road again in no time.

Off we sped toward Montrose thru the mountains and on roads that neither of us had been on before. We arrived in Montrose around 5:00 and again started the search for a hotel room. And of course, a simple task was made difficult because there was a club softball tournament in town that weekend. So the same challenge existed finding a room as what happened in Steamboat the night before.

Our problem was solved by the good folks at Motel Six. After a good night's sleep, I packed our things on the bike and got ready to head home. Our route was going to take us through Gunnison, over Monarch Pass, into Salida, Canon City, Colorado Springs and then home. Between Montrose and Gunnison there is a beautiful state park, lake and reservoir - Blue Mesa, which was extremely nice that morning. The sky was clear, temperatures were just right and the recent rains ensured that lake was high, which meant there were a lot of people enjoying the water and campground.

After passing thru Blue Mesa State Park and arriving into Gunnison, it was time for a break to stretch our legs and have something cool to drink. We found the local grocery store and we wandered inside to buy some juice and fruit. We sat outside in the parking lot and enjoyed the nice mountain morning and a quiet break.

We left Gunnison around 10:30 and continued along the magisterial sweep of Colorado's picture-perfect mountain highways. Our route took us over Monarch Pass into Chaffee County. By that time, it was getting close to lunch time, so I thought we'd check out what Salida offered in the way of food. After that, the story left our hands, and became one of family, fear, and that awful helplessness that one feels when loved ones are in danger but outside of our power to help. The first person to receive a call was Robyn's mother, Bonnie.

Sunday, July 18th

HI — IS THIS Bonnie Rupiper?"

"Yes it is . . . "

"This is Carol Johnson from Heart of the Rockies Hospital in Salida, Colorado. Your daughter Robyn has been in a motorcycle accident and is in our emergency room. She has a concussion and will be just fine. Mark has more severe injuries and is being airlifted to St. Anthony's hospital in Denver, and we need to get a hold of some family to let them know what is happening. Does Robyn have anyone close to here to help her when she becomes coherent?"

"Well, her sister Brenda is in Denver; let me see if I can get a hold of her."

"What about Mark? Is there anyone we can contact?"

"Well, I don't know. I will have to try and find someone"

"That would be great – Brenda can call me here to get the details."

Bonnie hung up the phone and turned to her husband. "Gerald – Mark and Robyn have been in a motorcycle accident. Robyn is ok, but it doesn't look good for Mark. We

11

need to get a hold of Brenda so she can find out exactly what is going on. We need to try and find Mark's dad Zedo."

It took my mother-in-law a few times to finally reach Robyn's oldest sister Brenda. Brenda was on vacation with her husband Austin and wasn't in a mood to answer the phone. Needless to say, she felt pretty bad when she finally got around to checking her voicemail. In a near panic, she called her mother back

"Mom! What's going on?"

"They were in an accident in Salida. Do you know where that is?"

"Yes. How are they?"

"Robyn is in the hospital there with a concussion and they are taking Mark to Denver by Flight for Life."

"NO! NO! NO! OH MY GOD! WHAT SHOULD I DO?"

"A nurse left her phone number. Can you call her and get the details? I don't have any of Mark's family's phone numbers, do you?"

"No, but I will think of something. Let me call the nurse and get the details and I will call you back when I learn something. I guess I can call up directory assistance in Calhan and ask for ANY Glaser or for the Glaser Family Gas Company. That's really all I can think of right now."

After Brenda hung up, she ran outside trying to find Austin (out taking the dog for a walk) and get him up to speed.

"Robyn and Mark have been in a terrible accident. Robyn's in the hospital and Mark is headed to Denver via Flight for Life. Oh my God, what am I going to do?"

Austin followed her upstairs and started trying to reach Glaser Gas. Meanwhile, Brenda got on the phone with the Salida Hospital. As it turned out, Robyn was going to be okay; just a little road rash and a concussion. They did want to keep her overnight for observation though. Mark, on the other hand, was hanging on for his life.

"He's on his way to St. Anthony Central and should be there within the hour. Do you know how to reach his family? We would like someone there for him when he arrives. I'm going to be honest . . . it doesn't look good." The nurse wasn't pulling any punches.

"I don't, but I am going to try and locate them and will try and have someone there when he arrives . . . even if it's not family. Is this the number I can call for updates on his condition?"

"Yes. We will stay in contact with St. Anthony's. Are you coming down to be with Robyn?"

"I . . . I guess I will. I will be in touch with you."

With her mind racing, Brenda started packing up her stuff. She wasn't going to wait for anything else, just get on the road.

That's when Austin asked, "Where are you going?"

"I'm going to Salida."

"Stop! Let's think about this for a second! Koa and I have no way to get home. Who's going to be there with Mark? What about his family? We need to figure some things out before you get on the road."

After the fact, Brenda realized that she was in a kind of trance, but at the time she could think of nothing but reaching her sister. She wanted to be in both places at once and knew that couldn't happen. When Robyn woke up, if she was alone, she was going to freak, yet Austin was right: Mark needed someone too – maybe even more. Who could she send? Krischel! Krischel has been one of Robyn's closest friends from high school, and she and her family have remained very close to ours over the years.

Brenda called Krischel and gave her the news. She agreed to go to St. Anthony's immediately. Neither one of them knew why exactly, but someone *had* to be there. Krischel also offered to send her brother to pick up Austin and take him back to Denver so that Brenda could get to Salida and be with Robyn.

However, no one knew a good way to reach my family. The best lead Brenda had was the phone number for Janet. Janet and I had first met on a plane, somehow struck up a conversation and became fast friends. Both she and her husband, Todd, had always been there for me when I needed them, and this time was no different. She quickly got on the case, and started working to track down my dad.

By this time, I had arrived at St. Anthony's Hospital in Denver. With Janet searching for my father and Austin taken care of, Brenda started the two-hour drive to Salida. At one point, Janet actually called her and said that she should try and get Robyn released that night if possible. They were bringing in the clergy to perform last rights for me. At this, Brenda actually screamed into the phone and pulled the car off the road.

"Oh my God! I can't be the one to tell my sister that she just lost her husband. I can't take it!"

Janet tried to calm the situation, saying, "Just focus on getting her out of there. You've got to hold it together and get her back with her husband. No matter what else happens."

Brenda finally arrived at the hospital in Salida sometime in the evening. When she entered Robyn's room they both just looked at each other and started to cry. Brenda gave her sister the biggest hug.

"How's Mark? Where is he? Was he wearing his helmet?"

Brenda took a deep breath. "He's fine, he's at St. Anthony's hospital in Denver and yes, he was wearing his helmet."

Having a concussion, as Robyn was somewhat disoriented. Brenda waited with her for an hour while she repeated those same three questions again and again. Brenda could only give the same answers until a nurse interrupted them, asking her to step outside with an update on my condition.

According to what the nurse had been able to learn, aside from the broken ribs, the lung contusions and the bumps and bruises, my more serious condition at that time was my brain activity. Since Zedo was there, he had authorized them to insert two 'antenna' as they came to be known by our family – a pair of sensors, inserted into my skull with a pair of wire leads, only vaguely reminiscent of alien antenna that would measure my brain activity. They had inserted a tube down my throat and put me on a respirator. At the moment, I was stable but definitely in critical condition.

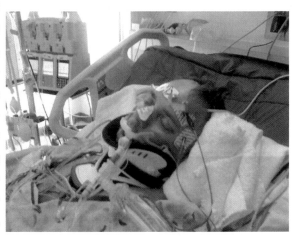

It was then that Brenda asked if there was any way that she could get her sister released that night.

"If Mark's condition worsens, they can request that the

doctor release her into your care. But right now, it's not likely."

It was frustrating, but Robyn also needed care that Brenda knew she couldn't provide. Worse, because of her concussion, there was a good chance that Robyn would simply be too confused to understand the situation anyway.

The nurse told her to go get some dinner and come back; "You need to take care of yourself after all."

Yeah right . . .

Regardless, she took her advice and by the time she got back, Robyn actually seemed a little more coherent. Her sentences were making sense now, but she kept repeating those same three questions. Brenda always answered the same way, never giving additional details because she feared that her sister just couldn't handle it yet. Robyn suggested that she call Damon, my boss, and give him an update since we were so close. It's important to point out that Damon and I enjoy a fairly unique relationship. He was really more of a mentor than a boss, and has really been responsible for guiding me professionally.

Damon wanted details that Brenda didn't have of course, but quickly arranged to be on the next flight to Denver. According to Brenda, she'd never heard a grown man cry like Damon did upon hearing of my accident.

When she got back into the room, it was time for a shift change for the nurses. It must have been around 10:00 or so when the new nurse came into the room and boy, was she excited. She introduced herself and stated she was the new nurse on the block. She then looked at Robyn and said, "And congratulations to you Robyn, I understand you're pregnant!"

Brenda was flabbergasted. She looked at the nurse with such astonishment that she sheepishly followed up with, "Uh oh, I guess not everyone in the room was aware of that!"

Just a week before at our annual BBQ, Brenda had asked Robyn if she was pregnant. She had looked her straight in the eye and said, "No, not this time."

Brenda's response, given the circumstances, was only natural. She stared at Robyn, and simply said, "Oh my God, you lied to me!"

Robyn must have been waking up because her answer was surprisingly lucid. "Don't you tell a soul!" she said, "I want this to be a surprise, and when Mark is better, we are going to share this news together."

Brenda agreed, and felt a little privileged to be the first to know. Her lips were sealed. That poor nurse . . . she'd let the cat out of the bag.

That night she spoke with David on the phone and got the update. He told her that I was stabilized, in a coma, and they were hopeful that I would make it through the night. David insisted that Brenda stay the night with Robyn and in the morning, he wanted to meet her at the front door with Robyn so he could prepare her for what she was about to see. Mark wasn't in a good place and he didn't want Robyn to freak. With a plan in place and her parents on the way (thanks to a friend with an airplane), all that remained was to get Robyn released in the morning.

The next morning Robyn was scheduled to be discharged at 10:00. That gave Brenda enough time to go to the police station and collect our personal effects and get the details of what happened. Up to this point nobody actually knew. Brenda was able to speak with the deputy who was on site at the accident and get a report, and she was able to share the information with me later.

On their way to Denver, Robyn was a nervous wreck. Brenda kept the details to herself, partly because she wanted Robyn to hear them from someone less emotionally involved, and partly because she didn't really know anything yet. Regardless, it was most important that Robyn be with me first. That would make it easier. So Robyn kept her promise to Zedo, and met him at the door of St. Anthony's with her parents.

And so began the second day of many more to come, but the one thing Brenda kept holding on to was that we were going to have a baby... everything was going to be just fine. It had to be!

Sunday, July 18th, 2010, Denver

BRENDA HAD MANAGED to get in touch with Krischel and gave her the short version of events so far. At this point, no one had figured out how to contact my father, Zedo. Fortunately, Krischel had kept an earlier email and was able to send a message off to most of our friends and family.

While Krischel headed to the hospital to meet me, her husband Sean headed to our house and met our housesitter Wes. When Wes answered the door, it was clear from Sean's face that something was wrong.

"Hi . . . I'm Sean, a friend of Robyn and Mark's. They have been in an accident and we need to see if we can find a number for Mark's dad. Do you have it? Do you know where we might find it?"

"I have no idea – but I can check in his office. Are they OK?"

"I don't know much. Just that Mark is on his way to St. Anthony's. We really need to track down his father. I guess it's pretty serious."

Sean only knew that I was being transported to St Anthony's in Denver by Flight for Life so he left Wes his phone number. He asked Wes to call if he found anything, and he left for the hospital.

Wes looked through my desk, in the closet, under notes... everywhere. Then it dawned on him to check the computer (I always leave my computer on, and before the Olympics, Robyn told me to type out a list of contact names and numbers). So looking at my computer desktop icons, Wes found a list of names. There it was . . . my dad's phone number.

Wes called Sean and gave him my dad's phone number, then he called Chris Martinez, one of our company branch managers to tell him what was going on.

When I arrived at the hospital, Krischel was the only person there to handle the questions that the St. Anthony's staff needed answers to. A nurse sat down with her in order to get as much medical history as they could manage.

"Are you related to Mark?"

"No."

"How do you know Mark?"

"He is married to my best friend Robyn."

"Do you know if he has any family here in Denver?"

"No, he doesn't. We are trying to get a hold of his dad."

"What is his medical history? Smoke? Drink? On any medication? Any past surgeries?

No – No – I don't know, and I don't know."

"Do you have any information that we may need to treat him for his injuries?"

"No. How is he?"

"Not good . . . we need to get a hold of family."

In the meantime, email notifications started going off everywhere.

My best friend Stephen read the email on his phone. He was at City Park for the Sunday Jazz in the Park Event. Stunned, he headed for his car. He drove towards St Anthony's hospital, but overwhelmed by emotion, had to stop a couple of times on the way.

When he arrived at St Anthony's, he was met by Krischel and Sean. They told him that I was in a motorcycle accident and that for the moment, I was stabilized, but they didn't know anything else. The doctors and nurses couldn't tell them anything because they weren't family.

Todd and Janet arrive next and wanted to know how I was. Of course, the answer was the same.

Janet though, had a few strings to pull. She was no stranger to state politics and bureaucracy, so She called up the El Paso County Sheriff's Department, explained what had happened, and requested that a deputy to find Zedo – he had to be at the Calhan airport or at his house.

A Calhan deputy went to my father's house . . .

In the meantime Todd, who was an attorney that practiced medical malpractice law, listened to the briefings from the doctors and nurses, and updated everyone else. Todd was a good person to have around, and understood what was going on, asked the right questions and updated everyone. The doctors weren't sure what to make of him and kept asking if he was a physician.

While combing over the details of my accident and condition, a priest walked into the room carrying my helmet. He had one simple question: who could take my personal effects?

A hush passed over the room. Was I still alive?

Sunday, July 18th, Calhan, Colorado

AIRPLANES AND FLYING have been part of our family since the early 1900's. My grandfather and his brothers began flying at an early age and have owned many airplanes. Grandpa gave flying lessons to others in the Calhan community and was drafted into the Army Air Corps during WWII. After the war, he continued to fly and taught my dad and both my uncles as well. The Calhan airport was established at its current location in 1974, and was where I learned to fly. As it happened, Bob Carpenter had just left my dad at the airport, and was driving by when he saw the deputy at Zedo's house. It was really a matter of luck that he decided to go back to the house and see what the officer needed.

"Hello – I'm Bob, are you looking for David?"

The deputy was watching Bob pull up, but relaxed a bit at the question. "Yes I am . . . do you know where he is?"

"Yea . . . I just left him. He's at the airport. Follow me, I will take you there."

The sheriff's deputy followed along behind Bob until the two men arrived at the Calhan airport. It's little more than a dirt strip, but had been serving the needs of private flight enthusiast for many years.

Bob honked his horn and signaled to Zedo. "Hey David! I was driving by your place, and this deputy was knocking on the door looking for you."

Deputy Johnson stepped out of his car and nodded to my dad. "Mr. Glaser?"

"Yes?"

"I am Deputy Johnson with the Calhan Sherriff's Department. We received a call from a Doctor Robinson at St Anthony's Hospital. He needs you to call him ASAP."

"OK – do you know why?"

"He needs to talk to you about Mark."

Meanwhile, a telephone started to ring in the hospital in Denver.

"St Anthony's Hospital emergency, how may I help you?"

"This is David Glaser and I am trying to find Dr. Robinson."

"One moment sir . . . "

"This is Dr. Robinson, is this Mr. Glaser?"

"Yes it is."

"Sir – Mark has been in a motorcycle accident and has suffered some pretty severe injuries. We are still doing our evaluation, but he definitely has a brain injury and several broken bones in his neck and chest. We are still evaluating all the injuries, particularly the brain injury. Can you get here in case we need your authorization for anything?"

"You said you are at St Anthony's hospital in Denver?"

"Yes sir – let me have you talk to the nurse."

The duty nurse took over the call. "Mr. Glaser?"

"Yes?"

"Is there anyone else here close who can drive to the hospital?"

"No – I'm the closest and will head that way right now."

Over the next few hours, my father got busy and contacted everyone in the family that he could think of: my brother Chris and his wife Vicky, my mother, friends, uncles and cousins. Over the coming weeks these people would become the core of my support group – constantly coming and going, and forever helping and providing whatever our family needed to help us get through my ordeal.

Once the family was notified, my father got himself to Denver. After he arrived, the hospital staff was able to bring him and our family and friends together to discuss my exact condition.

Doctor Robinson, a trauma specialist, filled them in. "I'm Doctor Robinson . . . we spoke on the phone. Mark was in a traumatic motorcycle accident as I explained on the phone. It doesn't appear that there is any immediate brain swelling, which of course is good, but anything can happen. X-rays were done in Salida that showed brain bruising, a break in two vertebrae and several broken ribs . . . we will further evaluate for other injuries, but those appear to be the worst. Because of the chest trauma, both lungs have collapsed, so the doctor in Salida inserted a tube into his chest and drained a liter of blood from the right lung and placed him on a ventilator. Once stabilized, he was loaded onto our Flight for Life Helicopter and transported here. In speaking with the flight nurse, breathing became labored and blood pressure started to drop during transport, so she inserted another tube to drain more fluid. Once he got here, our evaluation suggested that the left lung was also having difficulty and may contain fluid, so we inserted a tube in there. We drained a little bit of fluid, and now his breathing is consistent."

"What is the prognosis right now?" my father asked.

"I don't know sir . . . it's too early to tell. Things are breath to breath at the moment. I would say there's about a 5% chance of him making it thru the night."

"When can I see him?"

"I can take you in there now."

Zedo walked in to my room, where I was hooked up to many machines. It was a cacophony of noise, and made it hard to tell what any individual piece of equipment was doing. The nurse joined him and explained my condition and what the doctors were saying and doing. Every minute is crucial, and right then all anyone could do was wait.

"He doesn't have any swelling of the brain, but does have broken vertebrae in the neck. We won't know the extent of brain damage or if there is any paralysis for a while because he is sedated heavily for his pain, and also to keep him as still as possible because of the spinal injuries."

Many more family and friends showed up through the evening, but the hospital staff were trying to keep the number of people going in and out of my room limited so that I didn't become stressed. As a result, most of my family members were left to congregate in the empty waiting room at the end of the hall. My mother Nancy was one of the last to arrive.

Since a number of new family members had arrived, another doctor stopped by to explain my condition to my mom and my brother, Chris. The latest development seemed to be that the staff had inserted what is known as an ICP, or Inter-cranial Probe into my skull in order to monitor my brain for signs of swelling.

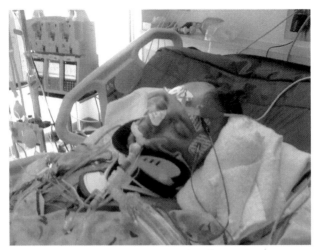

By the time the latest round of explanations were wrapping up, Zedo came back into the waiting room and saw mom.

"How is he?" she asked him pensively.

"He is breathing, but not doing very well. He's unconscious and on a ventilator. The doctor said he broke his neck and may have spinal cord damage."

"Can we see him?"

"Let's tell the nurse that you're here."

My mom was led into the trauma room to see me and immediately started to cry. Through her tears and in a voice that was more commanding than pleading said to the doctor, "I'm not losing another one!"

You see, our family was no stranger to tragedies like this. The year before, while Robyn and I were on our honeymoon, we returned to our room after a day at the beach and the pool to start getting ready to meet some new friends. I received a disturbing message from my father: my brother Shawn had been driving home from an all-day get together with his friends and ran off the road in his pick-up. It was early on Sunday morning when this occurred, and Shawn had fallen asleep while driving.

He had drifted off the side of the road, and when he corrected the wheel, his truck started skidding down the road and into the ditch. The truck was still going fast enough that when it went through the ditch, it jumped through a rancher's fence and landed on its top, rolling a couple of times before coming to a stop on its wheels only a few feet from the rancher's front door. Like I said, it was early in the morning, so nobody was awake at the house and there wasn't any other traffic on the road, so Shawn's truck wasn't discovered until later that morning. The impact broke Shawn's neck. He died instantly.

If the doctor was surprised at this, he said nothing. He spoke simply and professionally. "Mrs Glaser – he is stabilized and we just have to wait and see. The EMT report states that he was mumbling and responsive to pressure at the accident scene, so that is a good sign. We have him sedated right now so we can monitor his breathing. The ventilator is working to help his breathing because we don't think he can breathe on his own because of the chest trauma. We are going to monitor him closely thru the night and will update you on any changes."

After these crucial moments, the story became one of our family and friends providing us with more love and support than we would ever be able to repay. Some stayed for whole nights to help care for my family and simply be there for themselves. In times of great stress, sometimes those simple acts of love can make all the difference in the world. For my own part, I remained oblivious to the events unfolding around me.

Thoughts and Comments by Stephen
Monday July 19, 1:30 am – sent by email

Mark and Robyn Glaser were involved in a motorcycle accident yesterday afternoon near Salida Colorado. Details are not available other than that they were hit by a car and that they were wearing helmets.

Robyn suffered a severe concussion and other injuries and was taken to a local hospital. She has been able to talk to her sister who has been by her bedside, she is aware of the situation, and she is expected to be discharged later today, perhaps by noon.

Mark is in critical condition - he suffered broken ribs on both sides with associated damage to lungs / swelling / possibly incapable of breathing on his own, a broken neck / vertebrae, severe head injuries resulting in swelling and pressure, damage to his right shoulder, and other injuries. He was flown to St Anthony's central (17th ave near Sheridan in Denver) around 3 pm or so. He was awake and moving his limbs upon arrival - good sign. Only 1 hour of emergency surgery, but they continued to work on him in the neurological ICU until mid evening. His vitals have remained strong, but the problem with breathing, getting oxygen into his blood stream, and the brain injury are of great concern. They have done a limited cat scan, but can't move him to do a complete scan until they know if there is more damage to his spine, and can't test the damage to his brain until he comes out of an induced coma. It is not completely known how long he'll be in a coma, or the full extent of injuries, nor the outlook for recovery.

More than a dozen friends were at the hospital by 7 pm, and his family arrived shortly thereafter.

I'm staying the night with his dad Dave.

You may recall that Mark's brother died in a car accident just 16 months ago.

Week 1

St. Anthony's Hospital

The First Steps

Monday morning, July 19

I AM ALIVE!

When everyone wakes in the morning, there is a palpable relief that nothing had gone wrong during the night.

In the meantime, Gerald and Bonnie head to the airport and call Brenda along the way.

Robyn and Brenda are waiting for the doctor to come in and discharge Robyn from the hospital. She is getting frustrated, which means that Brenda is also getting mad . . . she doesn't show it, but she is.

Nevertheless, Brenda and Bonnie are able to get in touch with each other and have a quick phone conversation.

"Hi Brenda, how's Robyn?"

"She's awake and a little sore, but wants to get going. We are waiting on the doctor who is supposed to be here anytime now. Anything new about Mark?"

"No . . . we haven't heard anything – so I guess that is good. Krischel called late last night and said that all of Mark's family was there and they were just waiting for any news from the Doctor. I asked her to call me if she heard anything, and said that I would call her when we left here. We talked to Zedo and said we would be there tomorrow."

The doctor finally arrives to talk to Robyn and discharge her from the hospital. She and Brenda get in Brenda's car and head towards Denver, about three hours away. Along the way, Brenda gets continuous updates from the hospital, and every time the phone rings, she prays that it is good news.

Gerald and Bonnie arrive at Centennial airport in Denver, and Austin is there to pick them up. He takes them directly to the hospital and meets Zedo, Mom and everyone else in the waiting room.

Zedo tells Gerald that he would like to tell Robyn what is going on, if that is okay. Zedo and Brenda have several conversations that morning while Brenda is driving Robyn to Denver. He has asked Brenda to call when they are close so he can meet them at the entrance and tell her what is going on.

Robyn and Brenda arrive at the hospital around noon and are met at the door by Zedo, Gerald and Bonnie. Zedo asks Robyn to sit down so he can tell her what is going on.

Zedo explains all of my injuries and that I am stabilized in the Trauma room. He tells Robyn that I don't look the same and to be prepared. Robyn cries a bit; tells herself that she is going to be strong and not cry in front of me. And they head to my room.

Stephen meets them just outside my room, where Robyn and Stephen share a long hug and tears. Robyn goes in by herself as she wants to see me alone. Zedo, Gerald, Bonnie and Stephen all wait outside the door.

I am hooked up to the breathing machine, have tubes inserted into my head, a huge black eye, several scrapes and compression cuffs on my legs.

Robyn grabs my hand and starts talking to me. She whispers that she is okay, the baby is okay, and that she loves me. The nurse is standing there and sees my numbers go down, meaning that my breathing rate, heart rate and blood pressure have dropped.

The nurse tells Robyn, "you have to stay here . . . these are the best numbers we have had."

Dr. Robinson comes out and joins the waiting family members. Already tensions are high, so the silence is immediate as they listen to what he has to say.

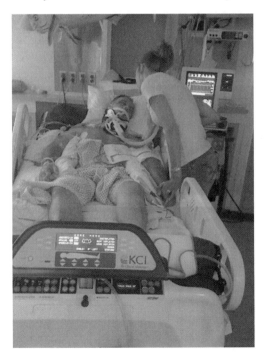

"I just saw Mark and he made a great first step making it thru the night. We are going to continue to monitor him and treat the injuries as we can. Right now we have him sedated and can't check responsiveness because of the sedatives. X-rays show breaks in the neck in two separate locations, so we will have to wait and see if there is any paralysis. The X-Ray also shows a hematoma located at both the right and left front sides of the brain. This could affect the ability for the brain to function properly and responses to be impaired. It could also explain the difficulty breathing, but we will have to wait and see. We have to wait until his breathing is stronger before we can start reducing the ventilator use."

To pass the time and chronicle the story for myself and our family, Brenda knows of this website, called caringbridge.org. It is a site that people can post their stories about a tragedy or illness and update people's status. Anyone can go to the site and read the latest developments. Brenda opens the website, starts a webpage for us, and writes a quick overview of what happened. She tells all the family and friends about the site, which will allow everyone to see the same information, instead of asking the same questions over and over.

Tuesday July 20, 2010
Caringbridge.com by Brenda

On Sunday, July 18th, Mark and Robyn were involved in a motorcycle accident in Salida, CO. Robyn incurred a concussion and was admitted to Salida Hospital. She was dismissed on Monday, July 19th in the morning with only bruises and scrapes. We are thankful that her injuries were not more severe.

Unfortunately, Mark suffered critical injuries and was airlifted to St Anthony's Central in Denver, CO. Mark is currently in a medically induced coma in the ICU due to the nature of his injuries. Although he is making progress, please keep him in your thoughts and prayers.

Robyn didn't leave my side for several days. Gerald and Bonnie stayed at our house and took care of our dogs.

Damon saw how tired Robyn was from sleeping in the waiting room chairs, so he stopped and bought an air mattress for her to sleep on.

Friends bring food . . . Krischel brings pillows and blankets; Brenda stays with Robyn to help her with anything.

The food that Janet brings is out of the ordinary for her as she is a vegetarian. But knowing how much I love red meat, she has decided to make a sacrifice and eat meat herself. She had written on my dry-erase board that she was going to start sacrificing animals and eat meat in support and would not quit until I got better.

Every day Janet would make it a point to come to the hospital to visit Robyn and see how I was doing. It didn't matter if it was for a few minutes over lunch, after work or during the day. She would make time and bring food for Robyn and our family when she could. We love you Janet!

Thoughts and Comments by Stephen
Wednesday, July 21, 2010 4:32 AM

An update on Mark & Robyn Glaser's motorcycle accident:

Please excuse grammar & typos - it's 4 am. To answer a couple questions first...

Can you do something?

- *Nothing is needed like food, but your presence will be needed soon. Mark will be in perhaps 3 weeks and we will need visitors after the initial rush of family and friends quiets down. Visit as often as you can, especially after this week.*

Where should you send cards or ???

- *Either to the hospital St Anthony's Central (call them*

for instructions) or their home (cards) - There is a CSC (Mark's employer) guy staying at their house to watch the dogs.

Why am I not responding to your calls and e-mails?

- It's too damn hard emotionally for me. I am telling Robyn you called / e-mailed / text ... and what your msg said.

Is someone with Mark?

- They don't let us stay in his room all the time, but otherwise so many family and friends are in and out and a couple of us prefer to be in his room a lot.

How is Mark's dad / family?

- They just suffered the loss of a son / brother 16 months ago. I saw Dave (dad) as he arrived Sunday night, no words, long embrace, tears. I've known Dave a long time, he always hugs me, says little about emotional stuff, but I know he's a caring man and deeply loves his kids. This is almost too much to handle. He is why I did not leave the hospital Sunday night. Going into Mark's room is very hard for him, he can only do a couple minutes at a time. Chris & Nikki (brother & sister) are strong in how they handle it. Both families are close to one another. When I first met Robyn's mom and dad it was as if you always knew them. Small town / country people, they know what matters - each other. It's no wonder why Mark and Robyn are so perfect for each other.

What do I need / how am I handling it?

- Thanks for asking, it means a lot. But I'm good, no needs. I spend a lot of time by his bed, preferably alone. I have my sorrow, anger. Don't like talking to anyone about him because I don't care what anyone *else thinks, hate the "cheer up" talk, hate the "it could've been worse" talk. I don't yet accept what has happened, struggle with how I see him laying there, but mostly, I'm afraid of losing him and am powerless to help him.*

THE ACCIDENT

On Sunday, approx. 2 pm, Mark and Robyn were on the 3rd day of a motorcycle trip through Colorado, and were entering Salida. Highway 50 or 24. A pickup is heading in the opposite direction and turns left in front of them. Mark skids 24 feet and then the bike goes down and slides 34 feet. At 40 to 45 miles per hour, there was no time to avoid collision or significantly slow down the bike. Robyn does not hit truck - she has no memory of the accident. Mark goes into the side of the truck. Mark's body may have shielded Robyn. Driver stops, lots of people around. The driver takes full responsibility and says he did not see them. Local emergency arrives in a few minutes or so. Robyn goes to local hospital. Helicopter called in for Mark. I spoke to flight nurse, he said they arrived in 30 minutes from the call (came from Colo Springs or Breckenridge), 15 minutes to stabilize and load him, 45 minutes to St Anthony's - one of the very best neuro trauma centers in the Country. It's not certain Mark will survive at this time. Brain injury, broken neck, broken ribs, collapsed lung ....

The driver feels horrible, called Robyn's hospital / police often Sunday night and Monday.

The investigating officer said they would have both been killed if not for the helmets - which Robyn insists they wear or she won't ride. She saved their lives. It is also felt that laying the bike down saved them from hitting the truck while upright on the bike and thus being launched which would have been more severe.

The other fact that saved their lives was that the accident happened in a town where there was an immediate response and getting Mark to St Anthony's

ROBYN

She is sent to a local hospital overnight Sunday, concussion, lots of bruises, road burn on right arm. Her oldest sister who lives in Denver arrives in Salida Sunday evening. Horrible night away from Mark, doesn't quite understand it all, and a doctor is giving her bad news about Mark. She is released Monday morning and arrives at St Anthony's early afternoon. I was standing outside Mark's room when she arrived which was just minutes after her family arrived from South Dakota. It was painful. When we saw each other there were no words, just long hug, tears. She could barely move, hurting in so many ways. She has to go through this every time she sees someone. When she sees Mark, I can only say that it was her hell on earth and her pain affected everyone there including medical staff. That's the thing about this and why I don't talk to anyone (save 2 people) outside of the hospital - it's too hard to keep going over it. Some of you will understand you've been there.

She cried, seemingly to me, all day Monday. She would not go home Monday night. I'm amazed at how so many others step up and put their emotions aside and attend to her, attend to each other. Food, touches, smiles, laughter. Keeps the treasure of being alive in the atmosphere, for indeed, two lives were nearly lost.

Today (Tuesday) she is so much better. She sees Mark improving, his swelling going down and his cranial pressure

going down. Still, I see several times where she sheds tears. Sometimes when she is by Mark alone, sometimes in a crowd in the waiting room. Right now (4 am Wednesday morning) she is asleep on an inflated mattress in the waiting room, with her Dad 10 feet away.

She has a lot more pain yet to come her way, and possibly the worst of it - when Mark's injuries are fully understood and when he goes into surgery.

MARK

Mark's real / full condition is unknown. The only movement is a jerk every time the respirator pumps air in and then sucks it out. Because it's so mechanical, he seems so lifeless to me. So many tubes in his head and body. Others talk often about his condition and the medical staff has been so generous in keeping 20+ people informed. But I'm confused because I detect conflicts in reports from different medical personnel. I don't see swelling going down as significant, I see a body that will not respond and that is on a respirator and I see nurses working on him no less than every 5 to 10 minutes. I don't look for hope, I want results. I just don't know how to explain this. Everyone has their own way of dealing with this. To me, to be honest, I don't know if I care more about him or myself, I simply cannot manage the thought of losing this person and don't have a way to help prevent that from happening - I can only wait.

What doctors have told me is that his brain is damaged, it will heal but the extent of the damage and possible effects of oxygen deprivation are still unknown. Monday his brain was the primary concern, now it's his lungs, and then his neck. He cannot come out of coma until his lungs will function on their own. They try to slowly bring him out of coma which should cause the body to become aware and thus function. But he doesn't respond correctly so they suspend. He is strapped and has mouth guards in case he responds too quickly and tries to pull his respirator tubes out. It's delicate, micro steps, uncertain.

He has a broken neck, or medically, a fractured C2 vertebrae. It requires significant surgery and he will have pins and screws. There will be limitations to head movement henceforth. This vertebrae is near a lot of spinal fluid - another area could have included spinal damage. His head hit that hard. Brain, neck, so much damage. But that's not all.

There may be more cracks in other vertebras. There are several broken ribs, and major lung damage. I don't understand the lung damage, so can't explain why this is now the major concern now.

So much is unknown because they can't do cat scans or MRI or other tests because he has to be stabilized first and then he has to be able to breathe on his own - and the things that are in his body to help him stabilize and keep alive also prevent the tests.

Wednesday July 21, 2010
Caringbridge.com by Brenda

MARK HAD A great night last night. He is maintaining his vitals which will allow them to lessen the sedation so they can test his reflexes. This does NOT mean he will be able to communicate with anyone. Once the test is complete, he will be sedated again. This is to protect his neck injuries. They will also be putting him in a new bed today . . .one that rotates from side to side allowing his lungs to recover.

The nurse reminded us that everyone has good and bad days in ICU. Today was a good day but keep praying because he's not out of the woods yet. They will continue to need your support.

Feel free to forward this link to any others that you feel may be interested. We are trying our best to keep everyone informed.

Zedo has been sitting with me for hours and needs a break, so Stephen takes him to the Harley Dealership to see the bike and stop for a meal. He and Zedo reminisce about the trips that Stephen would take with me when I flew to events . . . the early days that we worked together. They both get emotional at times, but have each other to console the other. Despite everything that's happened, Zedo has stayed pretty positive about everything. At one point, he even quips that, "it could be worse . . . I could be talking to the coroner . . . but I'm not – we are talking with a doctor."

Robyn wakes up in the middle of the night and sees Zedo lying across a table with his head on one chair and his feet on the other with his hat covering his eyes. She laughs to herself as that is all she can do.

Wednesday July 21, 2010

Caringbridge.com by Brenda

SORRY SO LATE everyone. Some of you may have heard that yesterday Mark had a slight set back at the end of the day. The medical team tested his ability to lie flat on his back for at least 30 minutes to see if he could be stable through an M.R.I. Although he fared very well through the test, his lungs were pushed to the limit and required him to be placed on a more aggressive ventilator. This machine is not very comfortable for the patient (or for the people watching it) and therefore requires increased paralytic and sedation meds. They also were unable to put him in his new bed which we were hoping would heal his lungs more rapidly. However, he again amazed us and had a stable night, so they switched him back to the old ventilator. This allowed them to reduce the paralytic and sedation meds. This led to a much needed uneventful day. The night ended on a high note when he made slight movements with his feet. We don't want to read too much into it at this point but it sure makes it easier to sleep tonight. Tomorrow is yet another day.

Hours come and go . . . days go by . . . nothing real new. The doctor tells Robyn that they can't do a CT Scan of my brain and neck until I can breathe on my own without the ventilator for at least 30 minutes.

Damon has been great, but it is time for him to go home to Los Angeles. He comes into my room with Robyn for an emotional goodbye. She thanks him for coming and for all his support. The conversation starts to become emotional and both Damon and Robyn start to cry.

Gerald and Bonnie need to get back home and run their business, so Kristi (Robyn's sister) makes arrangements to fly to Denver from her home in Iowa. Kristi spends several days and Robyn loves having family around to talk with. Kristi goes with Robyn to the first baby doctor appointment. The doctor is shocked to hear the motorcycle story and tells Robyn that everything is fine.

After several days, the doctors and nurses gradually start taking me off the breathing machine for a few minutes at a time and see gradual progress.

Thoughts and Comments by Stephen - 4:44 PM

Hi All,

Here's my update on Mark Glaser. A couple notes then Mark's condition.

NOTES

1. *Please excuse spelling & grammar.*
2. *Send cards / things to their home. Flowers, food, etc NOT allowed in his room. He is in ICU, it is not a recovery room.*
3. *If you visit, don't be afraid to just be there. You don't have to talk, in fact, Robyn would not mind some time not having to "host" visitors. That said, come by & just be there if you so desire.*
4. *If you visit, PLEASE be sensitive in your words to*

Robyn, hard for her to hear people's opinion about how bad Mark looks. If you see and want to discuss his condition that way, please talk to me.

5. E-mails and text are better than calls except for close family / friends - that way we can get to them when we are in the mood and it keeps phone open for critical calls.

6. It's nice having people around, just stressful having to discuss / update people over and over throughout the day.

7. Robyn's parents left Thursday, they and other sisters will be back in a couple days.

8. People are having to get back to matters in their lives, so the days of having 20+ people around most of the day are gone. That's fine actually, but will be nice to have more people around when Mark comes out of sedation.

9. Mark's family is fine, this seems most difficult for his dad Dave. Dave & I spend a lot of time together, suffice it to say that the pain is in his eyes and it's very deep. He enjoys his time driving back and forth to Calhan so he can experience his thoughts and emotions alone.

10. Nobody needs anything, and that includes Robyn & Mark's home and the dogs.

11. Robyn wants someone at the hospital 24 / 7 so if you'd like to do an "overnight", let me know.

12. Please excuse me & others if we don't get back to you soon enough - this is still a critical situation, often still very emotional as Mark has good and bad moments. However, and sorry I didn't know sooner, Robyn's friend Krischel set up a website for daily updates http://www.caringbridge.org/visit/markglaser

MARK'S UPDATE

He is still in the neurological surgical intensive care unit, he is still unconscious, he is still critical. Every day, every moment is all about his lungs getting stronger.

On Wednesday they removed devices from his head that were providing data on his brain and watching his internal cranial pressure - this is good because it meant the doctors no longer had critical concern about the stability of his brain. They also had him flat on his back for 30 minutes - which was great because that meant they could do an MRI, which they scheduled for 4 pm. But then one of his lungs stressed which resulted in its full constriction, so he had to be put on a different respirator that would keep his lungs fully expanded and do short rapid breathes which kept Mark in a constant jerking motion. Wednesday was a very bad day.

Hard on Mark, and hard to see him that way. Lots of tears that day. Fortunately it was my night to stay over so I was able to spend quiet time with him and the great part was that he was so peaceful that night. Most nights are not that way. You know what's interesting is how people in Mark's condition can sense and respond. He, via his vital stats, reacts differently to people. Guess who calms him the most. Yep. Robyn.

Thursday Mark went back onto his regular respirator, a very good sign. Since then it's just been a matter of him very slowly healing and dealing with challenges. Coughing, pneumonia, stress, etc. His life all depends on his lungs. To be frank, his lungs make it - so does he. Visa versa.

Yesterday they got him off the paralytic drugs and put him on a heavy sedative. So he's essentially still in a coma like state, but on the sedative the body becomes more aware of itself and its condition. This can lead to adverse reactions by his body (and it does) but it has to happen so the body can start healing itself aided by medical science.

This morning Mark was hiccupping, kind of hard to watch because the constant jerking does not help him. After awhile his nurse prepared medication to help him with the hiccups. While she prepared, Mark got a bit wound up. Stats shot up here and there causing concern. She comes in as well as a couple other nurses who have had Mark for a day, his nurse for today takes in the data, consider options including calling assistance and while I watch my fear and emotions follow suit and I lose composure, Robyn - she has stronger faith ... and then just as fast everything quiets down AND the hiccupping stops. The medical explanation from the nurses and doctor - Mark got pissed off with the hiccups and fought them off. Today is a very good day.

The Brain. It's stable, but they still do not know the extent of the damage because they still cannot test. It most likely suffered oxygen deprivation from the trauma of the accident which because of the severity of multiple life threatening injuries would likely have caused the blood flow to constrict and deprive the body of oxygen. Further deprivation most certainly has come from the extreme damage to the lungs which has been the most severe life threatening injury.

The Neck. Nothing new. They cannot operate, only stabilize. It is not good that this severe injury remains untreated (surgery) but there is no choice at the moment. Per my question Mark's neuro doctor said he could not guarantee that there is not any spinal damage, and no idea how much Mark's head movement will be permanently restricted.

The Lungs. Simple. They heal and he lives. The docs say lungs are very resilient, but the damage was even more severe than their resilience. It's all about using medical sci-

ence to help his lungs get to a point they can do their thing - breath and heal.

The Ribs / Other. Several broken ribs, tissue damage, and frankly, more unknown than know because they can't do the testing (most importantly the MRI).

The NSICU medical staff also take excellent care of Robyn and Mark's dad. They have an incredible tolerance for all the visitors. I am personally very grateful to them all because I like to be in his room the most but I am never kicked out even outside of visiting hours and though I am not family.

They hope is to get an MRI as soon as possible, next day or two. Two other majors targets are to do the neck surgery and to awaken Mark. This coming Wednesday is a big target day, but I forget why.

Dave (Mark's dad) and I went to the Harley yesterday to get personal belongings. Didn't bother us like we expected. The damage is minimal, and that was a big surprise. It just looks like it fell over going a few miles an hour. It obviously did not crash into the car that cut of Mark & Robyn. It's very hard to figure out what happened. I have my theory based on my riding experiences and motorcycle accidents I've had and others I've seen. Suffice it to say here that it so often comes down to how one falls. Robyn will always believe that Mark took the punishment and saved her - the evidence is strong in supporting that conclusion.

Thanks to all of you for the calls, texts, e-mails. I pass along your comments and save all the e-mails for Mark.

I received an e-mail from Brian C, a friend that managed parking for the Rockies back in my days there. Mark knows Brian as well, and we got together for dinner the last time I flew with Mark to Fort Worth to visit TCU (one of Mark's clients) back in March. Brian noted an even greater appreciation for that experience now. No mention of comparative tragedies, no need to mention that we hope or know Mark will recover fully. Just noting the appreciation that we have each other, and that we matter to each other, and in saying nothing, that we expect to do again. Many times. Now you knew why I fly with him and why I wanted us to see you. Thanks Brian, it's the first time the tears were more for joy than sorrow & fear.

Saturday July 24, 2010
Caringbridge.com by Brenda

*N*OT TOO MUCH *to talk about today and I guess that's a good thing. Mark's lungs continue to be the main focus because until they can work on their own, he is in a holding pattern with any other "repairs", and this will just take time. The doctors continue to balance all the critical pieces, i.e. lessen the sedation so he can continue to heal on his own while keeping him stable to protect his neck injury and keep him comfortable. Today Robyn and I got to see his CT scan from Sunday when he arrived at St. Anthony's. Although we still don't know what's going on in there, the doctor stated that his injuries didn't appear to be severe. They put him in his new bed today which will assist in lung repair so he can get to the next step.*

Thank you all for your thoughts and prayers. They appear to be working in our favor. Let's keep them going!!

Finally after the second week, I start to breathe better and can withstand short periods of time without the ventilator. The doctors schedule a time to take off the ventilator and have the CAT scan on my brain and neck done.

The CAT scan is done, and the results show the bruising

of the brain, and exact breaks in the C2 and C7 neck bones. There have been responses in both legs, both feet, both arms, both hands and pupils. Great news! There's still no certainty that there will not be some level of paralysis, but there is hope.

A well-respected neurosurgeon has been assigned to my case since the beginning and wants to start taking me off my medication. He wants to start an evaluation of the brain injury. As part of the process, he comes in one day and starts yelling into my ear . . .

"Maaaarrrrkkk" . . . nothing.

"Maaaarrrrkkk" . . . still – nothing.

Robyn starts to get mad and gives Dr. Jacobs funny looks. The doctor tells Robyn that my medicine is being reduced and I should start to wake up.

Dr. Jacobs tells Robyn about Craig Hospital, a rehabilitation facility in the Denver metro area that is one of the finest in the world. He has already been in contact with Craig and is waiting for a bed to become available. Dr. Weintraub from Craig has already come to the hospital to meet with Dr. Jacobs and they evaluate my condition. They decide that the facilities and expertise at Craig offer me the best chance for recovery.

I haven't had any real nutrition for two weeks, so the doctor's insert a feeding tube through my nose, as it is time to start a diet of liquid food. They also have to continue monitoring the lung injuries and clear the junk that accumulates in my throat because I can't consciously swallow to clear it out.

So, two other procedures are scheduled. The first is the procedure to insert the feeding tube into my stomach thru my nose. This tube is pushed up thru one nostril, down the throat and into the stomach. An IV of food is attached to the tube and vitamins and fluids are sent thru the tube into the stomach.

The other procedure is to do a tracheotomy. This will include cutting a hole into my throat, placing a tube into it and part of the way down the throat. Having this 'trach' in the throat will allow me to talk, but also will allow the nurses to clear my throat with the yonker.

Posts on Caringbridge.com from
July 24 – August 19, 2013 by Robyn
<u>Saturday July 24, 2010</u>

MARK HAD A rough night last night. He hates having a machine breathe for him so he's fighting the ventilator. This causes his vitals to fluctuate and that's the scary part. However, the respiratory doctor stated that he has the capability to breathe on his own but they keep him on the ventilator because they want him to expend his energy on healing instead of breathing.

They removed one of the drainage tubes on his right lung today because the fluid level is going down. They continue to test his reflexes each day. Although he's not responding it's not causing concern. Not all patients respond to this while sedated.

The "spine doctor" visited today and just made some slight adjustments to the way he is lying in his bed. The doctor stated that the vertebrae has the capability to repair itself but that is not the ideal solution so we continue to wait until his lungs improve, then they'll do an MRI to see what's REALLY going on in there, then surgery to repair his vertebrae.

Have a great day everyone!!

Stephen and I are best friends, and he hardly leaves the hospital. He is in my room quite a bit, and will do anything for me. One day while Stephen is sitting in the room, my toes move! Holy cow! Stephen is excited and lets everyone know. Robyn and the nurses come in, and Stephen tells them that I am waking up. The nurses tell him not to get too excited as it may be a muscle twitch. He doesn't care what it is . . . it is something. He stays in my room for hours and stares at my toes to wait for another movement.

Week 2

St. Anthony's Hospital

Sunday July 25, 2010

ONE WEEK AGO today, Mark was brought to St. Anthony's in critical condition and today . . . he's breathing on his own (with ventilator support). What a week! Of course, he still has many long days ahead but he is indeed breathing on his own.

He made small movements with his hands and feet today too. They've also increased the rotation on his bed and we hope that will loosen the "junk" in his chest and allow him to breathe better and heal faster.

It's more of the same story in that they continue to push his progress. Today when they decided to allow him breathe on his own, one of the nurses was quoted as saying, "go big or go home!" It's scary but we're confident that he's in good hands and glad they push him to heal on his own.

We all want the old Mark back.

Monday July 26, 2010

WELL SINCE MY last report, Mark ended up being a turd. He decided he didn't enjoy his sponge bath last night and his vitals escalated which required him to go back on the ventilator. The doctors were planning to take him off of it today but since it was so traumatic to his system, they changed their mind. They are trying to keep the sedation to a minimum and he's definitely responding to things like baths, changing sheets, etc.

There were some positive moments today too. He raised his arms and even opened his eyes for a brief second and more than once too.

They've decided to put him on a food supplement that's administered through his IV instead of the feeding tube because he's fighting that too. He hasn't had much nutrition since he's been up here and he needs his strength. They now want to do a CAT scan of his lungs when they do the MRI. They will leave the drain tubes in his chest until then and will be giving him a medication to try and purge fluid from his lungs.

It seems as though he has the most struggle during the evenings and that's usually when they move him the most, so they changed his schedule and did their maintenance during the day and sure enough . . . he responded. That's OK, responding is good at this point!!

Tuesday July 27, 2010

THIS HAS BEEN the best day of all since Mark arrived. We finally got to "see" Mark. He is slowly being taken off sedation. This smaller dose has allowed him to open his eyes and respond to visitors. It was so great to look him in the eyes and tell him we love him. He was also able to respond to commands (move your right toe, etc.). This was really exciting!

Mark is still on the ventilator, but the goal is to keep weaning him off and hopefully do an MRI tomorrow. This now gets tricky, as we want him responsive, but we do not want him feeling pain. He is so strong, but also pretty banged up. Right now, I imagine everything hurts.

Please continue to pray, as Mark is truly being touched by them all. Hopefully tonight goes well for him and tomorrow we take on another mile of this marathon!

Robyn's older sister Kristi is in my room when I start to open my eyes . . . oh the excitement. She calls for the nurse, and goes to find Robyn. They can't believe it is finally happening . . . I am waking up.

Wednesday July 28, 2010

LOTS OF BIG things are happening and I think we would expect nothing less of Mark. Today he was again opening his eyes and had some slight responses, but is still pretty heavily sedated.

He was finally able to lay flat on his back for an extended time, so tonight he had an MRI, a CT scan, and ultrasounds done. These will give us more information about his head, neck, chest, and abdomen injuries. We should have the results by morning.

It is so great to be able to see Mark's eyes open, and talk to him, but this also makes visits more difficult, as Mark gets more anxious. It also makes going home at night difficult, as now he knows when I am not there. They tell me he won't remember, but that doesn't make walking away any easier.

Thank you for all the thoughts and prayers. Keep them coming!

Thoughts and Comments by Stephen
Thursday, July 29, 2010 12:13 PM

Update on Mark Glaser since my last update Saturday July 24, 2010

- *For those new to my updates, all previous emails are below for you to read bottom up.*
- *please excuse errors, I'm not checking and my spell check is not working ...*

After I sent my e-mail to you last Saturday I went back to the hospital and sat in Mark's room awhile as I prefer to do. Over a 2 hour period I noticed his nurse was a bit stressed, she couldn't get Mark to relax. Then in a flash he started to struggle with breathing, his vitals went from 170s over 90s to 257 over whatever and climbing rapidly, his body and chest went crazy. She called a couple other nurses to help, then they called for a doctor, then a critical care response team, then I left the room. I saw Robyn heading in and told her there was a problem and that we were now blocked out. We watched people and equipment fly in and out. Robyn's tears were pouring, she was in fear and pain, hard to see someone hurt like that. I watched the entry to his room with an image of seeing this before at Red Rocks - when people fell off of the rocks and had those last convulsions before death.

We were asked to leave and wait in the waiting room. 30 or more minutes later a nurse came in to tell us all was well.

His lungs had accumulated too much mucus (?) and needed special equipment to clean it out. And so it goes. Up and down. Sunday was a great day. Mark's lungs started to breathe more than the respirator, and he was relaxed. In fact his pressure came down to 120s and 130s over 60s and 70s. We were all excited as perhaps he turned the corner, the lungs were healing and gaining strength. But that lasted only a short while, and again, back on paralytic drugs and full respirator, back to the starting line.

It's hard. Every day is a battle for an inch. He is constantly adjusted, trying to reduce paralytic or sedative drugs so his body can become more aware and heal itself, and trying to get his lungs to get stronger. For some the ups and downs wreak constant havoc on their emotions. For me, each little battle won or lost is a sign that he is fighting, and after all, he is fighting to stay alive.

Monday and Tuesday were much of the same. Gains and losses. Nothing as alarming as Saturday night, nothing as joyful the first Wednesday or this past Sunday. Just more back and forth.

Then came Wednesday (yesterday). I got in at 7 am as usual to relieve the overnighters - his mom and sister Nikki. When I went into his room, his eyes were partly open. He was aware. His nurse came in, Shari who was his nurse Tuesday as well, and she is full of spunk. She goes right into working on Mark, talking to him and asking him to squeeze her hand, move a toe, and then asks him questions - and he ever so slightly nods his head. This is beyond anything I imagined and of course brought tears to my eyes. Could not believe it. I thought he couldn't reach consciousness until the respirator tubes were out of his throat. But here we are.

I find out later that Robyn had this experience the night before after I had left. So in the few hours I had with Mark, and when his nurse said it was OK, I would talk to him and ask him questions - getting a slight nod for yes and a facial gesture for no. All answers correct, he was alert, he knows what's going on, recognizes voices. Good stuff.

I left mid day Wednesday because I would be back to do the overnight. When I returned around 9 pm, I could tell his *eyes moved more, his toes moved more, and we was staying awake longer. Even better, Robyn told me that they were able to get him down to do the MRI finally. In fact, he was able to stay flat on his back for testing for 2 hours. This was huge. Getting this testing is crucial and it also means that his lungs are getting better and that his body is handling it's condition better. This morning they said test results gave them a lot of crucial information and I didn't listen for the details while they were giving it all to Robyn, but I did understand that although there are very serious and critical injuries and a surgery or two ahead, there were a couple of things the spine doc was happy to see in those tests / MRI.*

I left a couple hours ago to take care of a couple things, clean up, and send this e-mail. Can't wait to see how's he's improved by the time I get back.

I know it's corny, however you will likely understand having seen miracles in birth or people overcoming tragedy, but how amazing can a simple body movement be when we truly honor and cherish the value of human life and something as simple as a smile - including one to yourself (which is easy for me because I am the coolest person I know).

Have a great day, and ponder that value.

Friday July 30, 2010

SO SORRY THAT nothing got posted yesterday. Let's just say that yesterday was Robyn's bad day. Mark continues to make improvements every day. He is still responsive, we are just not sure what he is understanding and remembering. That will come as the meds continue to decrease.

The big news of the day is that they have begun to wean him off the ventilator. He was breathing on his own for almost three and a half hours. This was awesome, as they only thought he would go two hours. Then they put him back on for the rest of the day and we will start again tomorrow. He is working hard for this because he wants that tube out of his throat!

The MRI came back pretty much as we expected. The C2 and C7 have injuries. For now we are still weighing our options as to what method of treatment we will choose. We have time, as nothing can be done anyway until the chest tubes are removed and his lungs heal a little more.

We are making daily progress and that is all I ask for right now. I will feel much better when the ventilator is off and out of his throat. I need to hear his voice!

Robyn

Saturday July 31, 2010

*T*ODAY WAS UNEVENTFUL, *which is always a good thing in the ICU. Mark slept most of the day (much needed!), but it means he struggles sleeping at night.*

He is moving more and more which is good, but that means we need to get his neck stable.

Hopefully Monday or Tuesday we can get that halo on so he can start moving more.

He was able to breathe on his own for two hours today. Hopefully tomorrow he can go longer. He is much more comfortable when he is doing his own breathing.

He is at his goal for tube feeding, so that makes me happy and him REALLY happy.

I want to thank everyone for all the support and prayers. I am not sure what the family or myself would do without all of you. Thank you for respecting Mark's privacy during this time of healing. This is a tough time for him right now. He tires easily and is frustrated with his situation. For this reason, he is not always up for seeing people. It always works best if you stop by the waiting room first and then someone will check if he is up for visitors. It truly varies day to day and hour to hour as they are pushing him pretty hard.

Today is the Junior Livestock show sale in Calhan for the County Fair, which we would normally attend. The Fair has been held in Calhan for over 100 years and I love to go for the sale. The Glasers have been part of the fair for most of those 100 years and always buy a steer or a hog from one of the 4-H kids. My nephews Chase and Bryce have shown lambs, hogs and steers for several years, and I began buying a hog every year a few years back. I have always loved giving back to the community and feel that 4-H is a great program for young kids to learn about farming, ranching and responsibility. The 4-H kids use the money to purchase an animal, raise that animal and send it to market in the future.

Chase has been very successful with his hogs and has won either Grand Champion or Reserve Grand Champion with one of his animals for several years. This year, Chase wins Grand Champion Market Hog and Grand Champion Showman . . . great accomplishments for anyone.

I, of course, couldn't go to the sale this year, but Zedo makes sure to attend like he always does. When Zedo goes into the sale building, everyone who knows him asks how I am doing. Zedo explains that I am making progress and that the surgery to stabilize my neck will be tomorrow. Everyone is relieved and wishes us the best of luck.

When Chase enters the ring, my dad bids for me in my absence. After a bit of back and forth with a few other attendees, he comes out ahead. Even the auctioneer gets into the spirit, announcing that Zedo has won the bid for me.

In the meantime, an orthopedic team has been keeping an eye on me so they can evaluate the treatment for the two broken neck bones. The primary doctor, Dr. Fouts, says that the standard treatment for broken neck bones is a 'fusion.' This process involves taking a piece of bone from the hip and attaching it to the neck bones. The process would secure the C2 and C3 bones together. Unfortunately this would reduce the range of motion that the head can turn from 80 degrees to around 40 degrees, but it would stabilize the bones so they can heal.

Dr. Fouts explains another process called a 'halo.' A halo is a brace that is attached to the head by screws inserted into the skull, and stabilizes the neck into a position that doesn't allow the head or any part of the neck to be turned. This will allow the broken bones to heal naturally.

However, because of the broken ribs and chest trauma, a halo will be risky and may not work. There could be too much weight and pressure on the chest.

Robyn and Zedo talk about fusion and they know that I would not be happy if I couldn't turn my head normally. I wouldn't be able to fly, I would have trouble driving, and I wouldn't be able to do all the things that I would normally enjoy.

But something has to be done, so it is agreed that the halo is the only option.

Week 3

St. Anthony's Hospital

Sunday August 1, 2010

WHAT A GREAT day today was. Mark is slowly getting back to himself. He may not be talking yet, but he is reacting; giving thumbs up, waving, winking, etc. What an amazing step from the last few days!

Mark did two hours of his own breathing today. Tomorrow they take the tubes out of his mouth and throat and leave a trach in that will come out his neck. They also will be putting him in a halo for his neck injury. This will be nice to get this going because he will be able to move more. Right now they are keeping him pretty still in order to protect the neck.

I can't tell you what a relief all of this is. Mark will be so much more comfortable, which, in turn, will make me more comfortable.

Tomorrow is a big day, so keep the prayers coming!

Robyn

Monday August 2, 2010

WELL, WE HAVE been saying what a roller coaster this whole thing is and today was no different. We were very excited to get into surgery and get the halo and the trach today. Unfortunately, that did not happen. There were so many traumas brought to the ICU last night and today, that Mark got bumped. This was understandable, but very frustrating, especially for Mark who was anticipating a kiss on the lips and maybe even a little ice cream!

So here we sit, hoping tomorrow will be the day. They better get that halo on soon because as you all know, Mark does not sit still. Today he attempted, multiple times, to pull himself up. He is also determined to get out of bed to use the bathroom. Not happening!

Hopefully tomorrow will be the day for surgery so we can begin to work on getting Mark out of that bed. This will put both of us at ease!

Love you all
Robyn

Tuesday August 3, 2010

WE HAD HIGH hopes for surgery today. We sat around and waited all day . . . while Mark slept. Finally, at 9:30pm they finally rolled him in for trach surgery. The halo will not be put on until tomorrow. That is disappointing, but we will wait. Other than that, not much new news today. Waiting for news on the surgery, I will let you all know tomorrow.

By now I am awake, and the doctors want me to spend time sitting up so infection doesn't develop in my lungs. If that occurred, I would have to go back on the ventilator. At this point, I also have my days and nights switched, and all I want to do is sleep during the day. Robyn keeps me awake and sitting up in bed. I apparently don't like this and start getting mad at her.

The nurses keep pushing me to stay awake and sit up in bed. The doctor tells Robyn that I need to be helped out of bed and sit in the room chair. I don't like doing this, but Robyn makes me.

I like having the TV on so I can watch the news. But I am still very tired, and fall asleep with the TV on. When I awake, I keep turning on the Spanish channel, but quickly fall asleep again. The nurse asks Robyn if I speak it because I keep turning on the Spanish channel. Robyn tells the nurse that I speak very limited Spanish and can't understand why I keep settling on it. Later, they figured out that the next channel after the news was Univision, and I couldn't manipulate the remote more than a single click.

Thursday, August 5

*S*ORRY FOR THE delay on updates, things have just been a little crazy. The trach is going well. It is taking Mark some getting used to, but each day is a little better. He was breathing on his own today for seven hours. This was amazing. It is very difficult, but he is pushing through. He is still not talking, but started trying today. At least he can mouth words, and I got my first "I love you" in a long time!

The doctors have decided that they are not going to put a halo on Mark. Based on X-rays, the C2 fracture is remaining stable, so they believe the collar will be enough. This is great news! Now we don't have to worry about the vest on the halo constricting his lungs and broken ribs.

The best news of the day is that Mark sat up on the edge of the bed. It was exhausting, and really hurt his ribs, but it was a start. He is stronger than I ever imagined (and I knew he was strong).

This whole ordeal is really testing his mental strength and patience, along with mine. We are leaning on each other to pull through each day. Our next steps are getting him off breathing support and out of ICU. Each day we get a little closer.

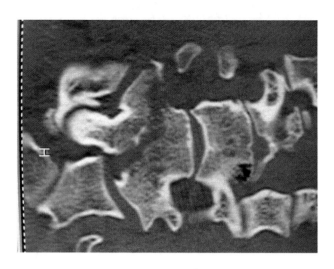

The days continue to pass, and Dr. Fouts leaves for vacation. His colleague, Dr. Henderhiser is handed the case. Dr. Henderhiser reviews the chart on Monday and checks my reflexes and responses. He believes that a stabilization collar should be sufficient for the bones to heal and tells Robyn that an x-ray will be done weekly to make sure the bone is healing properly; if it isn't, then the fusion surgery will have to be done.

Robyn tells Doctor Henderhiser that she wants an x-ray done every few days. Dr. Henderhiser tries to explain that an x-ray won't be required that often, but she insists.

And it was a good thing that an x-ray was completed, as the next day, the x-ray showed that the factured C-2 bone had moved 6mm: a significant change for such a sensitive area.

Thoughts and Comments by Stephen
Friday, August 6, 2010

Hi All

An update on Mark Glaser since my update last Thursday (7/29).

- *My previous e-mails are below (read from bottom up) if you are interested.*
- *This will be my last e-mail to this group, if you want me to update you again in a week, please be sure to reply back to me and I'll put you on a new list.*
- *You can also follow updates posted by Robyn and her sister and friend @ http://www.caringbridge.org/visit/markglaser - I think this is updated daily.*

Last Thursday Mark began to open his eyes, ever so slightly, and would just stare straight ahead. He likely didn't see anything, this was just his body "awakening" as the medical staff reduced sedatives and amnesia medication. He also started to move his arms and inch or two.

His lungs are improving but this is still the big challenge. Every day he has to work hard to breathe on his own as much as he can to strengthen his lungs. Remember, all but a couple of his ribs were broken ("crushed" has been used to describe it) and the lungs were so severely traumatized they could not function on their own. The good news today is that they have taken him off of the "old" respirator that included tubes going down his throat, and did a tracheotomy (sp?) on him which provides much more comfort (it's a very standard procedure) and will allow him talk in a day or two.

Objective through the week-end; his lungs breathing longer on their own. Next week; Craig hospital reps will visit him to check on his progress and talk about when he can move to their facility for rehab.

By Saturday his eyes were completely open and he would

try to look to the left or right, but mostly just stared straight ahead. Arm movement increased, he could lightly squeeze his hands, some foot movement. You could tell he knew people were around, and that he was trying to move limbs.

Throughout the days and nights there would be times where he seemed comfortable and times he

was not - mostly because of breathing challenges, coughing, medication, and the medical staff always trying to get him to breathe more on his own. This continues to be a challenge to today.

Overall, he turned the corner last week, from survival to recovery. During the last several days Mark has improved in awareness, moving limbs, facial expression, breathing on his own. He communicates by nodding, facial movements, pointing, and writing on a pad. Doesn't remember the accident but everything else, he can't talk but you know he is all there and he is the same 'ol Mark - he even smiles and jokes via gestures and that eyebrow raising thing he does, and he recognizes everyone who comes by.

His recovery will be long but he makes remarkable progress daily. Appears there is no brain damage. An MRI showed a fracture in his neck at the C2 vertebrae and damage to the C7 -

HOWEVER, they decided not to do surgery because it had the risk of permanently reducing head/neck movement by up to 50% or, I also heard 80%. Instead it was decided to put him into a halo for several months. HOWEVER, he has been healing so well that now it's been decided to just keep him in his neck brace. This is a major upgrade in his recovery plan as it will provide him with a much better quality of life during the next several months - and it is possible he may achieve close to or perhaps 100% healing and use of head / neck.[end of Stephen's comments]

Friday, August 6

ANOTHER ROLLER COASTER *ride today. Mark had a great day. He is still breathing on his own (since 8:30 am), and we are striving for midnight. He also was able to get up and sit in a chair today for a few hours. All of this was great news.*

Unfortunately, the spine doctor came in this evening and informed us that since Wednesday's X-ray, the spine fracture has moved 6mm. That is scary and means that they will now be doing surgery. The surgery is scheduled for Sunday morning and the plan is to fuse C1, C2, and C3. Obviously this makes us very nervous, but we have to trust the doctors.

Please keep praying. This was tough news and we could use all the extra prayers to get us through.

Robyn has told Dr. Henderhiser the concerns she has about the fusion procedure and asks him to think of another option.

Dr. Henderhiser thinks about it – consults another surgeon in his practice, and they determine that an instrumentation stabilization process that is common care for lower back injuries, could be an option. He explains this process to Robyn and Zedo, and highlights that doing this process will be an experiment as it has never been done in the neck region. Robyn wants to think about it before she approves the surgery.

Robyn calls several friends to ask their opinions. She calls Dr. Anderson (our chiropractor friend) . . . she calls Damon . . . she discusses the procedure with many more friends and all the family.

She asks Dr. Henderhiser to explain the procedure to me so that I can understand what is going on and the risks associated with this surgery. He comes to explain everything to me, and as soon as he finishes, I point to the door, and mouth, "Let's go!"

Dr. Henderhiser schedules the surgery for the next day.

Week 4

St. Anthony's Hospital

Sunday, August 8

WELL, SURGERY WAS successful! Everything went great and Mark is now sleeping sound. He is very sore, but that will pass. The surgeons seemed very pleased with the procedure and now we wait six months and see if the bones begin to fuse themselves. If they do, then we can remove the hardware and Mark will maintain full range of motion. This is good news!

We have jumped another hurdle and glad it is done. Thank you for all the extra prayers to help us get through the surgery. I am making sure to tell Mark about all the positive thoughts going out for him.

Monday, August 9

MARK HAD A tough day, as now the hard work begins. They are now starting some therapy and it is not easy. Today they got Mark to the edge of the bed and he was able to stand and pivot himself to sit in a chair (with support). This was exhausting!

He sat in the chair for four hours, which he was not too happy about. He was tired and sore and wanted to go back to bed. I told him that I was the boss now and I want out of ICU just as bad as he does, so he needs to push through. He made it, but he was tired.

I was really a bully today, because I also forced him to stay awake all day. He has his days and nights mixed up, so he is not sleeping through the night. Hopefully we tired him out enough that he will sleep tonight.

Tomorrow we continue therapy and possibly try breathing on his own for 24 hours. This is a big, but necessary step to getting out of here and into a rehab facility.

Thanks for the continued thoughts and prayers. I have been filling Mark in about all the people that are asking and praying. He too, is amazed.

Love you all!

Tuesday, August 10

*T*HINGS WERE A *little uneventful today, which is never bad in the ICU. Once again, Mark was up and in the chair today. They got him to stand up straight, with some help, which was so good to see. Still breathing on his own since 10:30 this morning and shooting for going through the night. A nice day.*

Wednesday, August 11

SORRY FOR NOT updating for a few days. Not a lot of down time lately. Mark is doing so well, even though he doesn't always think so. Yesterday, he was up in the chair all day. It is so nice to be out of the bed! He also is officially breathing on his own and the ventilator has been moved from the room. Every time a machine or tube leaves that room, I smile.

Today, Mark had a big day. He was up and on his feet, and even did a little walking around the room. He also got his trach downsized which means they were able to put a speaking valve on today (still working on using it, but I got an "I love you" out of him). Tomorrow, they start training him to swallow, which means we are soon getting rid of the feeding tube and moving to the real stuff.

We are planning on being out of here Tuesday morning and moving to Craig Rehab. It will be a nice change of pace and scenery for both of us. We still have a long road ahead of us, but moving out of ICU is a huge step.

Not sure how we would have made it this far without all of you, so thank you so much for everything!

I am having difficulty going to the bathroom, but the

doctors aren't real concerned. They give me some medicine to help with the constipation. However, several days go by and nothing positive has happened, so the nurse has to give me a suppository.

When it is time for me to get up and move around, nurse Sherry has me turn around and she does a sneak attack. My hospital gown is open in the back, so Sherry inserts a suppository. I look at the nurse and mouth, *"I hate you"*. I don't really mean it, but say it anyway. Sherry laughs and puts me back to bed.

I am now getting better and can be moved to a room that doesn't require full-time attention. Dr. Jacobs and the rest of the medical staff are still not sure of the extent of my brain injuries, but all are positive that I am going to require considerable rehabilitation.

Thursday, August 12

WE ARE MOVING out of ICU!! Mark is officially making the move to a room on the floor tonight. We are very excited about this. Today was a good day. Mark is doing better at talking with the valve, still wouldn't choose it, but he can.

Today was another uneventful day. Mark is getting out of bed every day and attempting to walk around the room. Other than that, it is about keeping him awake so he sleeps at night.

I apparently didn't like being covered up in the bed, so I continually take the bed covers off. At times, I even take the hospital gown off . . . I get naked and start showing off the goods.

One day while Chase and Bryce are visiting, and while they are in the room alone with me, I take off my clothes and get naked. Brenda walks in and looks at Chase with a funny smile. Chase covers me up and I look up and tell Brenda, *"I'm hot! It's hot in here. I want a fan"*. Brenda tells the nurse that I am continually getting naked because I am hot and that I want a fan.

A fan is brought in, but now Robyn has to check and make sure that I'm not lying naked before anyone can visit.

Dixie is Robyn's younger sister and wants to come help her sister, so she arranges to fly to Denver from her home in Sioux Falls. Bonnie and Gerald want to return to see us as well, so they fly with Dixie from Omaha.

Dixie stays in my room one day so Robyn can have a break, and I keep trying to get Dixie to bring me a Powerade. I keep telling everyone that I want a Powerade and a turkey sandwich; I wasn't exactly sure why, but for some reason I had become fixated on the idea. Dixie has to explain to me that I am not allowed one yet, and not for the last time. I still have tubes down my throat and am being fed through the feeding tube. So until, I have those removed, no fluids or solid foods are allowed.

Saturday, August 14

SORRY FOR NOT posting yesterday. We had a rough couple of days. Mark has been very anxious and not sleeping at night. Now that he is out of ICU, there is no more one-on-one nursing. This makes me nervous, because he is uncomfortable and still unable to do so many things. For this reason, we have been staying overnight with him. He has been sitting up and trying to get out of bed, which is a great sign of his ability, but I am scared that he will try to stand up and he will hurt himself.

Last night was better, and he is much calmer today, so hopefully the new meds are working better. So far, the biggest news of the day is that Mark is getting his first actual shower since we got here. We are all very excited.

We are still on track to leave for Craig on Tuesday.

Monday, August 16

WE WALKED DOWN the hall today! It was great! He was happy to be up, and it just proved that we are ready to move to Craig rehab tomorrow. Mark is becoming more and more independent every day. I can only imagine how fast he will progress when he starts in rehab every day.

We make the move tomorrow at eleven. If you are thinking about visiting at Craig, you may want to call first or give us a few days to figure things out. We are unsure what to expect, but hear it is pretty intense. We know we have weekends free, so that is also an option.

I will continue to update the site, but thank you for all the thoughts and prayers during our time at St. Anthony's.

Family and friends are around me all the time. The support given is unbelievable and appreciated. Damon comes back for a few days to see how everything is going, and when he gets ready to leave, he comes into my room with Robyn to say good-bye. I am awake this time, and recognize Damon. When Damon says that he will see me again soon, and to get plenty of rest, I point at Robyn and make a motion over my belly. Damon isn't sure what I am trying to say, so I motion again. Damon figures out that I am trying to tell him that Robyn is pregnant. Damon smiles, congratulates us and tells everyone good-bye.

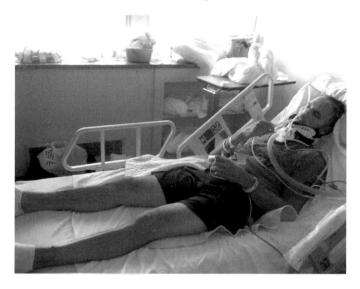

Week 1

Craig Hospital

Tuesday, August 17

WELL, WE MADE it to Craig rehab. It was a busy day of getting pulled in multiple directions to get acquainted with everyone. It is a great facility and I have no doubt that Mark will make great progress there.

We have a busy week ahead of us. Mark not only begins work with physical therapy, occupational therapy, and speech therapy, he will also be going through multiple assessments.

For this reason, please do not feel obligated to get up and visit. There is not any downtime in the day, other than sleeping, and he will need that. The weekends would be a good time to visit. There is no therapy.

Thanks for understanding and keep us in your prayers. This will be a long, tough road.

Wednesday, August 18

THE DAYS ARE Filled with many trips to therapy and testing sessions. I meet with Deb, the speech therapist, who is testing my memory, thought processing and reasoning. Deb quickly becomes a favorite staff member at Craig. She has a no-nonsense attitude and refuses to allow me to settle. She walks me through each phase of my cognitive testing and provides moral support during every step.

Dr. Berry is the neuropsychologist, who is also going to test my memory, explain the functions of the parts of the brain, and how the injury will have residual effects on deductive reasoning. Dr. Berry is candid in his approach, and while sometimes shocking, it is appreciated.

Occupational therapy is monitored by Jeanine, and she is going to teach me how to adjust daily activities to overcome any physical challenges. She works with me on how to become independent, so when I do get to go home, I can take care of everything myself.

Before I start the day of therapy sessions, a respiratory

therapist comes into my room to have me breathe through a ventilator with medicine. Like everything else, I don't really like it, but am learning to accept the demands of my treatment.

Wednesday, August 18

CRAIG IS DEFINITELY *different than St. Anthony's. I hate to say we are pushing visitors away, but he is rarely free. They have him going all day (right now mostly tests), and at night they really prefer they save their energy.*

Mark is still not sleeping at night. This is hard on both of us. The doctor thinks it has something to do with the brain injury, so they have asked that no one stay with him at night so they can figure it out. This is so hard.

Since we have been here, the brain injury is becoming more apparent. Keep this in mind when you visit. We have been advised to talk to him "normal" (volume and speed), but use less complex sentences.

We can also see the injury coming out through his lack of patience and some anger coming through. I never thought it would be this hard and I am only on day two here.

I just pray I have the strength to make it through this. I have no doubt he will pull through, it is just going to be a long road. Thanks for all the support.

Thursday, August 19

I WAKE UP early, but am very tired. I couldn't sleep because my days and nights are still mixed up, and between the neck collar and feeding tube, I have to sleep on my back. Because my lungs are still recovering, the bed is elevated. Every time I move, I slide down the bed a little bit. And because brain injuries often cause emotional and behavioral instability, the doctors are concerned that I may try and get out of bed by myself. As a result, I sleep in a Posey Bed. A Posey Bed has a net type enclosure around the bed. When I am in bed and by myself in the room, the tech zips up the sides of the bed, so I won't try and get out.

I am pretty aware of what is going on, and understand that I can't get up by myself. Being enclosed is simply making me aggravated. When I see Dr. Weintraub next, I tell him that when I do finally fall asleep, and the tech needs to leave the room, or returns, the bed is zipped closed or open and wakes me up. Between the feeling of being trapped and the noise, I'm having a hard time sleeping. Dr. Weintraub listens, agrees and asks the nurse to have the Posey removed.

I have several X-rays, tests and therapy sessions, but still want some water. It wasn't because I was thirsty, just that the act of drinking was akin to scratching an itch. Robyn stays with me during the day and goes to the therapy sessions. One of the meetings that I go to is with Dr. Berry. He tells me about my injuries and that I was messed up. He talks about what we might have to expect as far as memory loss and how to deal with the challenges.

He asks Robyn if she is ready for me to be different. This kind of shocks her and she doesn't really know how to respond. Dr. Berry explains that every Traumatic Brain Injury, or TBI, is different and each patient reacts differently. He goes on to say that there could be changes in things I say, how I say them, what I mean and how I respond. In all likelihood, I will probably be more emotional and less patient. He tells us that it normally takes two years for a brain injury to heal, and that there will be many hurdles and changes in that time. He also talks about changing habits. There are simply things that I won't be able to do anymore: whether it be riding the motorcycle or skiing. Falls and injuries to the head, even small bumps after a major incident like mine could be devastating. 20% of all TBI patients have a second injury in those two years, and they need to do everything possible to reduce the odds of having another injury. This means getting rid of the Hog, staying off ladders and the roof and learning how to allow other people to help me.

In the meantime Jenny, Robyn's youngest sister, has flown in from Minneapolis to help Robyn and visit. She is a great help and comes to the hospital to visit me. Brenda comes by tonight to visit as well, and brings Robyn and Jenny some food. Robyn feels bad for me because I can't have any, and offers to go out in the hall to eat. I tell them that it's okay, and want them to stay.

Thursday, August 19

TODAY WAS BETTER than yesterday. Mark was in a little bit better spirits and is showing improvement every day. He is up and on his feet with help, and they are keeping him busy in therapy.

Our biggest goal at the moment is to get rid of the feeding tube. Hopefully this comes soon. He is still unable to swallow, so they are keeping it in. He has another swallow exam tomorrow, so keep your fingers crossed!

Everyone here has been great. The people are all very nice, so that helps. Hopefully, the days continue to improve. Once they get him a turkey sandwich and some powerade he will be good to go!

Friday, August 20

ANOTHER FULL DAY of testing is ahead of us. Up to this point, I have been given a multitude of tests to measure my cognitive functions to baseline my treatment schedule. These tests become very frustrating as I am beginning to realize the effects of the brain injury – deficiency of short term memory, losing patience with menial tasks and growing mentally tired quickly. Deb has administered many of these tests, and she can sense my frustration.

Today when I meet with Deb, she tells me that they are going to do a Barium Swallow Test to see if I can swallow fluids. I have to pass this test before the feeding tube can be removed and I can eat. Deb explains that the procedure will consist of me sitting up in front of an X-ray machine and holding a barium solution in my mouth. I will then swallow the fluid and the X-ray will show the fluid is moving down the throat . . . they want to make sure that nothing goes into the lungs.

I listen and respond: "I'm not going to pass this test."

Deb: "Why would you say that?"

"I have a tube stuck in my nose and going down my

throat, and another tube in my neck going down my throat . . . I know I won't be able to pass this."

"Well, we have to try. We can't take the tubes out until we do this test and show that you can intake food and fluids without aspirating."

"OK – but I know I won't pass it."

I go back to my room and wait for Deb to come and get me for the test. A short time passes and the tech from patient transport shows up to move me into the wheelchair. Deb meets us at my room and we head to the testing area.

When we arrive, I find a small room with an X-ray machine and small video screen. I am moved up next to it and positioned to see the screen.

Deb explains that the screen will show my throat and how I swallow. The barium will show up as a dark "blob" on the screen, and they will be able to see where the fluid goes.

Deb hands me a small cup with some fluid in it and tells me that the fluid is barium. Barium is a fluid that is easier to view in an X-ray. When she tells me to take a drink, I am to take a small drink of the barium and hold it in my mouth. She will tell me when to swallow it. If I start to choke, I need to go ahead and spit the rest of the barium into the trashcan next to me.

Deb: "Ok – are you ready?"

"Yep – ready"

"Go ahead and take a small drink and hold it in your mouth."

I take a small sip and hold it.

"Are you ok?"

I nod yes.

"Go ahead and swallow – good . . . are you okay?"

Again – nodding my head yes.

We do this several times and record the results.

Deb explains to me that the fluid is bypassing the ability to hold it in my mouth, but it's not seeping into the lungs – good news.

When I return to my room, Robyn is waiting for me. We will have a meeting with the medical team later in the afternoon. She is joined by Zedo, who keeps her company while I take a nap. By mid-afternoon, I am moved into the wheelchair and we head off to the day's meeting.

In the conference room, Dr. Weintraub, Dr. Berry, Stacy, Deb, Nurse Lois, and Melissa have gathered to go over my progress. Dr. Weintraub starts the meeting by talking about the initial observation, and shows the MRI of my brain on a monitor. He talks about the bruising and the treatment schedule. He briefly describes what everyone will focus on and how I need to spend the next few days just resting. The beginning of the week will kick off the rehabilitation schedule.

Dr. Weintraub says that normal recovery from this type of brain injury would be 12 weeks, which would have a discharge date of around October 18, but based on the early evaluation and initial tests, my rehab would be 11 weeks, thus making the discharge date October 8.

I immediately say: "That's unacceptable!"

Looks of astonishment were on the faces of everyone, and Robyn leans in and says: "You can't say that."

Zedo just sits quietly and smiles to himself.

Dr. Weintraub glances at me, opens the chart, rubs his head and begins to write. He flips through some pages, and closes the chart. He then looks at me and says, "what about the first part of October . . . what does this mean to you?"

"That means September 30."

Dr. Weintraub opens the chart again, writes something down, and says, "Okay – September 30th it is."

I look around the room. Everyone is looking at me, so I explain my feelings. "Failure is not an option here – we have a lot of work to do. You can tell me what to do, but only I can make myself better. The best is yet to come."

Dr. Weintraub closes the chart and people start to get up. But I'm not satisfied. I have a few more questions for him.

"Should I be concerned with clots as the blood starts to dissipate and get absorbed back into the body?"

"Great question – we will monitor that and treat this with blood thinning medication."

"What about stroke? Is there a risk of stroke?"

"Another great question – we are also going to treat you with anti-seizure medication, and again monitor your behavior for this."

"OK – thank you."

Everyone leaves and Zedo pushes me back to my room in the wheelchair.

After going through another round of tests with Deb later that day, Deb can tell that I'm upset and asks if something is wrong. I am again struck by a sudden desire for a drink, and tell her, "I want a drink."

Deb pauses and says, "I'll be right back."

Deb returns with a bottle of cold Powerade, which I'd been asking about for days, and tells me that I can have a small spoonful and that Robyn is the only one who can give me this.

I have my first drink – it is only a spoonful, but it is the best thing I've ever tasted. It's been 42 days since I have been able to drink anything and I almost cry. Robyn pushes me back to my room for more rest, while I have a death grip on the Powerade bottle. I have a few more drinks, and Deb says that she will make a note that I can have small sips of water or Powerade, but that I have to use a spoon.

Dr. Weintraub comes in and also discusses the test results. He goes on to say that Deb believes that I can swallow okay, and that the only concern would be my ability to chew food as my jaw may have started to atrophy from disuse and my stomach may struggle to digest food. Dr. Weintraub says that they can remove the nasal feeding tube, but will have to replace it with a tube inserted directly into the stomach, or an upper GI tube, in case there is a problem eating and getting enough nutrition.

"Can we do it today?"

"I'm afraid not. There is still too much barium in your system."

"Can they do it tomorrow?"

"The doctors don't do these procedures on the weekends, as the operating rooms and staff are held for emergencies only. They will have to do it on Monday. Also, once this tube is put in, it has to stay for at least six weeks."

I'm not real happy and Dr. Weintraub can see it in my face. He continues: "I think you have this idea that as soon as you are allowed to eat, you will be able to eat normally. You won't be able to do that . . . your jaw hasn't worked to chew food in quite a while, and your stomach will have shrunk. Your body isn't used to solid food anymore. It's going to take some time to get that ability back."

I tell Dr. Weintraub, "Oh, I'll be able to eat!"

Dr. Weintraub says that the upper GI tube procedure will be scheduled for Monday, and then they will be able to take the nose feeding tube out: "Just be patient and don't get your hopes up too high".

We are introduced to a new nurse today, Sherry. Robyn and I both like her. Like everyone else at Craig, she is very compassionate, understanding, and easy to talk to. It is easy to see that she cares a great deal about her patients. In retrospect, I was lucky to have her as a nurse.

I tell Sherry that my chin hurts and ask her to look at it. She moves the neck collar around a bit to see what may be bothering me and sees an open wound where the collar has rubbed the skin away.

She tells me that she has to take the collar off for a moment and to not move my head. She removes the front piece of the collar and takes a picture. Everything is documented for my chart even though I tell her that there is nothing to worry about and it is just another wound. She insists on noting it and says that she is surprised that nobody charted it before.

Now that the tests and consultations are complete, Robyn tells me that she has brought all of my mail, the get-well cards and notes, as well as my computer and cell phone. The doctors have told me that I can start looking through these and that I am free to use my computer, but only for short periods of time. So I begin reading all the notes, cards, and Caring Bridge posts, as well as read my email and listen to my voice mail. It will take me several days to go through all of this, but I am truly shocked and appreciative of how many people took time to write and leave messages.

Jenny and Robyn leave to get something to eat and when they come back to my room, Robyn tells me that she doesn't feel well. She has cramps in her stomach and is worried about the baby.

The tech Paul is working again tonight and I tell Paul about how Robyn feels. He nods and heads off to locate the nurse. When he comes back with a nurse in tow, it is quickly decided that my wife should be taken off to the emergency room.

They leave me with Jenny, but it isn't long before Paul comes back and offers to take me to the ER in order to be with Robyn. After moving me into my wheelchair and covering me with a blanket, the three of us head down to be with Robyn.

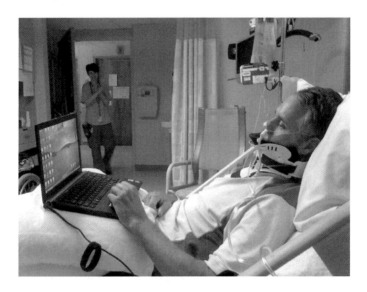

Robyn is in a room waiting for a doctor who shows up shortly after we arrive. The ultrasound tells us that everything is ok; the baby looks good and we have nothing to worry about. This is the first time that I have gotten to see the baby or hear the heartbeat; a sound that is emotionally overwhelming, yet confusing. Here I had just escaped death, and now we are bringing a person into the world. During my stay at St Anthony's, Robyn had made me aware

that the baby was ok, but I had no recollection of any conversation about the baby. Of course, I am still in a bit of a
fog and have to wonder if I really appreciate the wonder of
the moment as fully as I would have liked.

After breathing a sigh of relief, we go back to my room.
I am tired, so I lie back in bed and fall asleep.

Posts on Caringbridge.com from August 20 – September 22, 2013 by Mark Friday, August 20

*H*ELLO FOLKS - YES it's me . . . not time for me to go yet. The fine Dr's at St Anthony's got me repaired and patched in a way that I could move to Craig's Rehabilitation Hospital this past Monday . . . what a great next step. The folks at Craig are very determined and I have told each of them that I will be out of here in a couple of weeks. And of course, each of them have looked at me like I am crazy to which they either commented or said "No way - most people are here at least 4 weeks" . . . and of course my return comment is "I am not like most people - plan on seeing me off in a couple of weeks".

Unfortunately, we had a slight set back today as I planned on passing my swallow test today and getting rid of my feeding tube and start working on eating everyday solid food . . . believe it or not I am craving a turkey sandwich and powerade . . . I know - CRAZY!

Well, I didn't pass my swallow test, but the Dr's are still going to take out the feeding tube on Monday so I can work on training the throat muscles that control the food part of swallowing, which means I should get that turkey sandwich sometime Monday - Yeah!

I can't tell you how much it means to me to see the comments and words of support from each of you. Thank you for taking the time to write your comments and sharing your thoughtful prayers . . . yes, it does help lift a person's spirits.

Tomorrow will be another good day and more progress is on the way.

Thank you again for the comments and keep them coming. I will log on again tomorrow and provide another update.

Mark

Friday, August 20

ONE OF THE best things about working on this from a hospital bed is having the ability to sit here in my underwear and type what I want . . . I know there are some of you out there who sit in their underwear and not only read the postings, but also write your own from the comfort of your underwear -so keep feeling good about what you are doing . . . there isn't much shame or privacy in the confines of a hospital.

Saturday, August 21

HAPPY BIRTHDAY DAD! Zedo is 64 today. Otherwise, it's the weekend and everything is quiet around the hospital. I get to go outside today. It's going to be a great day!

A doctor from the orthopedics office comes to check on me and make sure I am comfortable with the neck collar and that nothing otherwise is going wrong. When the doctor arrives, he reviews my chart, and sees the note about the wound on my chin. He asks me how the wound happened and wants to take a look. I tell him I'm not sure, but that it itches. The doctor tells me not to move my head and he takes off the neck collar. He sees the wound and asks the nurse for a pair of scissors...he is going to do a "pit stop modification".

So the Dr cuts a piece of the collar off and opens the area near where the collar rubs on my chin . . . ooohhhh – much better.

I then ask the doctor if he would take the staples out of the back of my neck where the surgical incision is; they're itchy too. He asks when the surgery was done, which was less than 2 weeks prior, so the staples can't be removed yet. He tells me that they can be removed on Monday.

When the doctor is finished, Robyn asks the tech if she would help move me into my wheelchair. I want to go outside and sit in the sun; something I haven't done in six weeks.

I move into my chair and we go outside to sit in front of the hospital. Having the freedom to move from my room and into the world – fresh air, the sound of cars, trucks, mowers and nature, is something that we all take for granted. When that luxury isn't there, you begin to miss it.

Robyn tells me that Brenda and Jenny have gone to the house to check on things, and are bringing our dog Lady back with them, so I can see her. When they arrive, I can see Lady walking towards us in the grass, sniffing all the new smells, as she hasn't seen me yet. When she finally does, she is very excited and pulls Brenda as hard as she can against the leash, whining and panting with excitement to get to me. When Lady gets to me, she jumps up in my lap and proceeds to give me kisses. Her obvious joy at our reunion is just another step toward normal.

Despite, or maybe because of the excitement, I find myself tiring quickly and need to go back to my room. Brenda and Jenny take Lady home and I go back to my room to rest.

I lay down to rest and turn on the TV . . . there has to be a football game on somewhere. But I quickly fall asleep.

When I wake up, I tell Robyn that I want to take a shower. Robyn calls the on-duty tech, who says that she will have to see if there is a time available in the shower and that she would have to take me.

The nurse checks the schedule and sees that there is an available time at seven, and asks if that is OK.

I really want a shower, so I agree. Robyn stays with me, and we all go to the shower together. I can't be alone of course. It's difficult and risky to maneuver myself in and out of the wheelchair, and I certainly can't manage a shower on my own.

After so long though, the time in the shower is totally awesome. I have to sit in my chair for the shower, but what a wonderful feeling. Hot water splashing over my head from a showerhead, soap running down my shoulders and back, steam rising into the air, this again is something easily taken for granted.

Saturday, August 21

*H*OWDY SPORTS FANS - sorry I didn't update yesterday - not much to talk about. Weekends around Craig are pretty slow, which is very aggravating for me. They want their patients to use the weekend for relaxation and recovery—well, as far as I am concerned, it is a huge waste of 48 hours —let's get on with things.

Anyway, still have the feeding tube in my nose, which is extremely uncomfortable and agitating . . . but tomorrow is the day that it gets replaced and I can start working on re-training my throat muscles so I can have solid foods and beverages . . . only 28 more hours to that turkey sandwich and powerade.

I want to again thank each of your for the kind words and positive thoughts, but I want to especially thank Robyn for her perseverance and helping me stay positive. She is the true rock and leader in this whole ordeal. When you see her, I am sure that she can use a big hug and smile.

On a separate note, some of you already know, but many of you don't, but Robyn is pregnant (11 weeks) and the fetus was uninjured in the accident, so that is one more thing we are thankful for.

Not much going on today—some visitors (which is always nice) and some time outside. Robyn's sisters Brenda and Jennifer brought my girl "Lady" over yesterday and it was exciting to see her. It's been since the accident since I have seen her and it was cool. She was excited to see me, but those of you who know her, can understand her doggie ADD and how much she gets distracted with the different reflections, smells and sounds, but she still jumped up in my lap and gave me big dog kisses, which was much appreciated.

Well, I'm off to relax for the day and see what I can find to do on a weekend and will update the journal tomorrow—hopefully with a sandwich in one hand and Drink in the other.

I hope everyone has a great weekend and I look forward to seeing each of you in the near future.

Sunday, August 22

I DIDN'T REALLY want to sit in my room, so we all go outside again and across the street to the East building. There are other treatment rooms in this building along with the Therapeutic Recreation department, or T-Rec. The T-Rec is a room full of table games, and activities for the patients to participate in. Once a patient is stable, Craig has the staff and facilities to coordinate activities away from the hospital like fishing, boating, basketball and others.

Since it's Sunday, things are pretty slow in T-Rec, but there is a therapist in the room who shows us a few games we can play.

The one I like the most is a target game with blow darts. Not real darts, but Velcro ones that will stick to a target at the end of the room.

Everyone enjoys the time and I go back to my room. Nikki and her family came up today to visit. My niece Brittney made me a get-well card that I still have today. They are such good kids.

Nevertheless, I get tired quickly and need to lie down.

Up to this point, I don't really know all the details of the accident and the five weeks since, so I want to know more details and start asking Robyn questions: Where did the accident happen? How did it happen? Was anyone else injured? What were my injuries? What were your injuries?

"Well," Robyn says, "the accident happened in Salida, a car turned in front of us, and just you and I were injured. You had a lot of injuries – broke your neck, brain injury, which is why we are at Craig, twelve broken ribs and a broken scapula. Because of all the chest injuries, both of your lungs collapsed and you had to have tubes put in your chest to drain the blood and then put on a ventilator. You were taken by Flight for Life from Salida to St Anthony's. You were there for just about five weeks before you were brought here this week."

"What happened to the other Driver?"

"The police officer who investigated the accident called me and said that he was going to issue a ticket for failure to yield, but because of your injuries, he could also issue a citation for reckless driving if he wanted us to add that on, which could possibly mean jail time. Brenda and I talked about it, and knew this was an accident and having him go to jail would not change what has already happened."

"Good," I said. Not good that he got a ticket, but good that criminal charges weren't pursued . . . It was an accident.

Week 2

Craig Hospital

Monday, August 23

ANOTHER DAY OF tests ahead and it starts slowly. However, today is going to be the day that the upper GI tube is put in and I begin the steps to have the feeding tube removed from my nose.

I am transported to the operating room and wait for the surgical team to prepare. A few nurses and tech's stop to talk and ask questions in preparation for the procedure and wait for the Dr.

I have to keep things light, so I ask the nurse if they have an extra sharp scalpel.

"Why?"

"Because you have to cut thru abs of steel today."

Everyone chuckles - The doctor arrives and we all go into the operating room. While the rest of the operating staff gets ready, he asks what kind of music I like.

"Country."

"OK – is there an artist you prefer to listen to?"

"Hmmmm – how about Garth Brooks?"

"Let's see what we have."

Sure enough, Garth comes on and starts singing *Friends in Low Places.*

The procedure is underway, and the Dr tells me: "OK – we are getting ready to put the tube in, so don't burp. If you do, we will have a mess."

"OK – I'll try not to burp. Is it OK to fart?"

Again, the room chuckles and the doctor replies, "Maybe ok for you, but I don't think it would be good for the rest of us."

The procedure finishes without a problem and now I have a tube directly into my stomach. When I get back to my room, a dietician comes in and unhooks the food IV from the nose tube and connects it to the stomach tube. She tells me that the nose tube can be taken out and I will be monitored for calorie intake.

I want Nurse Bert to take the tube out. She was my first nurse when I got to Craig and I enjoy her personality and candor.

A short time later, Bert comes in and tells me that she can take the nose tube out when I am ready. Since I'm more than ready, I tell Bert to go ahead. Robyn is in the room and stands by my bed to help in any way she can.

Bert asks me how I want the tube removed – slow or quick and fast?

"Quick and fast – just pull it out . . . all at once . . . get it over with," I tell her.

Bert says ok and begins the process. She removes the tape holding the tube in place, and begins pulling on the tube. She pulls for a moment and the tube starts to come out. It becomes tight and Bert asks, "Do you want me to stop?"

"Nope – pull it out." I can feel the tube sliding out of my body, which is uncomfortable, but I just want this done.

Bert continues pulling on the tube and it is so painful, I

start to moan, groan and ultimately scream. Bert continues to pull on the tube and it is finally out; 68 centimeters of tubing about the size of a restaurant straw.

The tube has small barbs on it to keep from moving while in the stomach, and those barbs along with the tube itself, initiate my gag reflexes and I start to dry heave. Nurse Bert grabs a bucket in the room, and Robyn holds it under my chin.

Later that day, the dietician comes and tells me that Deb will set up a time for me to eat, and for now they would continue feeding me through the upper GI tube. She also tells me that I have to have three straight days of a calorie intake of 2000 calories or more. Once I can do that, then they can discontinue using the tube.

"So you have to keep track of everything you have . . . cookies, mints, whatever. We will check with you every night, so keep a list."

She told me that once I did start eating, I could have an evening snack, and asked what I would like.

Like I mentioned previously, I love my ice cream, so I ask if I could have a shake.

"Sure, what kind?"

"Chocolate? And while I'm asking, can I get peanut butter and banana in it?"

"We can do that. We will have it placed in the freezer down the hall every evening."

Part of the therapy includes two massages in my room at my bed. So the massage therapist asks me if I would like a massage (who wouldn't?), and she works on my back and shoulders.

I finally relax and fall asleep.

Monday, August 23

HERE'S TODAY'S UPDATE - may not sound like much, but it was pretty exciting for me. I had the feeding tube removed from my nose (yes - it hurt like a mother - 68 cm's long) and had a new feeding tube inserted directly into my stomach. Sounds disgusting, but what a relief - most of you know what is next (turkey sandwich and powerade by the end of the week - it's the little things you miss). Tomorrow is going to be another big day - I'm having my trach taken out, which will allow me to speak normally. Then it's just the rehab process - building muscle strength, brain rehabilitation and confidence - won't take me long though.

One thing that the Dr did request is my staying off work email and the work phone. I will still read updates and will communicate thru the corporate office, but please, everyone - do what you know how to do and manage the business. I will be back nipping at your ears soon enough.

Minor items, but certainly notable ones - thank you for keeping the notes coming and for those of you who have come by to visit - it's very appreciated.

Tuesday, August 24

STACEY COMES TO my room to get me for the afternoon session, and helps me to my wheelchair. Stacey tells me that as I gain strength, I can start using a walker, but not without the help of a nurse, therapist or tech. Agreed.

I really want to wash my face before therapy, so Stacey helps me to the sink and I turn on the water. I look at myself and my body in the mirror and tell Stacey that it looks like my chest is out of whack. I have always been an athlete and believed that I knew my body well, but what I was seeing was not my body. My muscle had withered away leaving me a wisp of my former self. My ribs are easily seen thru my skin . . . my shoulders are not square above my hips, my skin is pale, my face is shallow . . . I just wasn't me.

Stacey agrees that my body is out of whack, that my shoulders are rolled forward and that my chest is not square with my hips. She says that we will work on fixing all of that. With all the broken ribs and after lying down for so long, the spine has moved into a curved position. I remind Stacey that my shoulder still hurts and I know that it isn't just muscle pain.

147

Off we go to therapy, where Stacey has me lifting light-weight bags, holding myself up on the edge of a bed, and walking with the walker. I am very weak from not having food, or doing any activities for so long, so I get tired real quick. I have also lost 40 pounds so far, and Robyn says that I'm just skin and bones.

Stacey wants to work on my back a little bit, so while I am lying on the therapy table doing shoulder exercises, Stacey asks me if she can help me roll over and lie on my stomach. I am a little apprehensive as my neck is still in a collar and the doctors have been very clear that I am not to move my neck at all. Stacey knows this of course, and makes accommodations to support my head with towels and padding.

With Stacey's help, I roll over onto my stomach and try to get comfortable. There's not much comfort in wearing a neck collar and trying to lie face down.

I start to relax but get light headed. I tell Stacey and she responds by saying, "Just lie still and let me know if it gets any worse." Things even out and Stacey starts stretching my arms, shoulders and back. It hurts, but it's a good pain . . . muscle stretches that will feel better eventually.

Stacey shows Robyn how to use the gait belt and how to get me in and out of bed, and tells her that if I want to move about the hospital, she can help me.

Today is also the day the staples come out of my neck, and I've asked to have Bert remove them. When she arrives, she has me sit up in bed and tells me that she is going to remove the collar and start taking them out one at a time. Bert starts, and one by one removes the staples - 19 of them. Ahhh . . . much better. No more itching and something else removed!

Dr. Weintraub does tell me that they will be able to take

the trach out and the nurse will be in shortly to do this. He explains that it is a very easy thing to do and that the hole in the throat will heal naturally . . . no need for any stitches. The hole will close up in a few days.

This makes me happy as it is one more thing that will be removed from my body. And I will be able to talk normally.

Nurse Sherry comes in a short time later and begins taking the trach out. She cuts the stitches and slides the tube out. There's now a hole in my throat, but I immediately feel better.

Yeah! Another milestone.

But now a new hurdle: I haven't had a bowel movement since I got to the hospital. They have been giving me laxatives, and finally something is happening. But it happens before I can get to the bathroom. So needless to say, there is a mess to clean up.

I am so embarrassed, but my tech Holly, is very understanding and helps me out. Holly is still a student studying for her degree in speech therapy, but is very professional and friendly. She has been helping me get to my therapy sessions and keeping me company when Robyn can't be there. In the morning when I dress, she lets me wear what I want, even when it doesn't match.

I am still having trouble sleeping thru the night, so the doctor prescribes a sleeping medication. When I receive my medication at 9:30 every evening, I fall asleep by 10:00, but wake up around 2:00 am and can't go back to sleep. I'll usually take another pill and fall back to sleep, but have a hard time waking up in the morning.

Tuesday, August 24

GOOD EVENING FOLKS - what another great day it's been. First of all, I got a full night sleep. Haven't got my sandwich and drink yet, but I did have the trach removed (more tubes taken out - yeah!), and the respiratory therapist told me earlier that we are going to try the introduction of small food particles tomorrow - exciting!

Thank you all again for taking the time to write the notes on caring bridge, sending emails, and sending cards and notes of encouragement. I want everyone to listen real closely - never take advantage of your day or the people you love - you never know when it will be your last opportunity to tell your loved ones how much you do love them and how much you care about them.

The folks here at Craig Hospital are amazing. They come to work each day with a focus, remain positive and upbeat and always leave with a smile and telling me how good I am doing and what a great day I had. They are absolutely great people and if I started listing each and every one, I know that I would unintentionally forget someone, so I will continue to thank each of them every time I can.

Over 10,000 hits on the website . . . none of you know how much that means and how emotional that is for me - you are all great friends and I don't know how I can repay each of you.

I'm going to keep it short, as I explained in an earlier post, the Dr's want me to keep email and phone conversations to a minimum, but none of them understand how truly blessed I am to not only be here, but have the support that you have each given.

I will provide another positive update tomorrow.

Wednesday, August 25

EVERY MORNING, DR. Weintraub visits me between 7:30 and 8:00. When he visits today, I ask him if I can take all the medication except the sleeping meds. Dr. Weintraub says they can try it, but it is important to get rest.

I also ask Dr. Weintraub if it would be OK to walk around the hospital floor with a tech when I wake up in the middle of the night. Dr. Weintraub asks why. I tell him that maybe it will help me go back to sleep, and that everyone has told me that I won't be able to walk on my own until I regain my strength, so walking a little bit at a time will help build my endurance.

Dr. Weintraub agrees and makes a note in his chart. Dr. Weintraub also asks if I am still using the Yonker.

I use it on occasion, but don't think I need it anymore. Dr. Weintraub agrees and tells the nurses to discontinue its use. He also tells me that the respiratory therapist has noted that I am getting better with my breathing, so the ventilator sessions will be ending today.

By reading the notes and talking to the therapists, it sounds like things are good. Dr. Weintraub asks how my shoulder is feeling as my chart notes that there is still pain and discomfort.

I tell Dr. Weintraub that there is still some pain and definite weakness. It doesn't feel like normal muscle fatigue, and that something is wrong. His guess is that there may be some nerve damage and I will be scheduled for an EMG test later.

Uh oh – this doesn't sound good.

I finish a couple of therapy sessions with Deb, Stacey, Dr. Berry and Jeanine. I am finally starting to understand what is going on, and why it is important for me to be at Craig. I am starting to see that my memory and thought processes aren't as I remember them. My short-term memory is faulty. My attention span is diminished. My patience with small things is shorter. I tire more quickly. So it will be important for me to listen to the medical teams and apply myself the best way possible.

Every day, I am living with people who are much less fortunate than I have been. There are patients here who will never get to walk again – never get to pick up a pencil – never get to feed themselves, and some who cannot even speak . . . but not one of these people feel sorry for themselves (or at least show it) – they focus on their new path of life and make the best of what they have been afforded.

We all need to step back and have a little appreciation for all the things we take for granted.

Think about how natural it is to do the everyday things we do without a second thought – walk to the restroom, step into the shower, grab a glass for water, eat when you are hungry, put the key in the car ignition and drive, answer the phone . . . what if you all of a sudden you couldn't do those things? This is my new reality. I had never really considered how much a person might need the help of others.

Robyn had to go back to work today, but she comes by to stay with me in the evening. I tell her about the tests, but I am still annoyed. I tell her, "This whole thing sucks, but I would give about anything for Shawn to have had this opportunity."

My brother's death was traumatic for me and our family, but there's little enough Robyn can offer in terms of comfort. She simply says, "I know."

It is time for Robyn to go home and get her much deserved rest. She gives me a kiss, tells me that she loves me, and leaves for the night.

Wednesday, August 25

HELLO EVERYONE - ANOTHER great day. Didn't get to eat, but did have another tube removed and was approved to drink water - you don't know how good it tastes!

I also spent an hour with the physical therapist and we walked all around the hospital without my walker and did some testing, which indicated that I am not a fall risk and I can now walk the halls without a hospital assistant and without my walker (as long as my body can handle it).

The other exciting thing is that we may get approval for a day pass . . . which means Robyn can take me home sometime this weekend and I can see the girls and spend some time in my own environment.

Some of you have been inquiring about visits. I just ask that you call Robyn first to make sure I do not have classes or therapies scheduled and that there are not too many visitors at a time.

Love you all
Mark

Thursday, August 26

ANOTHER DAY OF therapy and I feel like I am getting into a routine, but I really wish that I could add food to the list of things I have to do each day. Everyone has been so supportive. I continue to read the daily messages on Caring Bridge and my email. Many are from friends, work colleagues and members of our church. While I was in the hospital at St Anthony's, I had many visits from church members who brought meals, cards and smiles to Robyn.

I ask Robyn if she would call Pastor Dave from our church in Greenwood Village and see if he would come to the hospital and give us communion. He agrees and comes to the hospital that night. I am glad to see him and we all chat for a while before Pastor Dave gives both Robyn and me communion. I ask if he will say a prayer of forgiveness to the driver of the car who turned in front of us.

Thursday, August 26

*H*I EVERYONE - ANOTHER *positive day (not as much as I had hoped, but still positive). I get to eat tomorrow and we were told that we would have to wait another week before we could get the day pass . . . a bit of a bummer, but the Dr's know best.*

Speaking of which, we had a good meeting with the Dr's today and they asked me to trust their timeline and program . . . and to be patient - not one of my stronger personality traits, but I told them that I would do the best I could.

Our friends Todd and Janet will love this one - I'm starting off with applesauce tomorrow and the speech therapist is recommending milkshakes as the next food group - so Ice Cream . . . who wouldn't work their fanny off for that?

Thank you all again for your support and I still see a lot of inquiries about a visit - which I would love, so coordinate with Robyn. We want to make sure if you visit, I am actually around. I spend a fair amount of time in various therapy sessions, and want to make sure that I am here and can spend time together when you do visit.

Talk to everyone soon.
Mark

Friday, August 27

ANOTHER DAY OF testing and when I meet with Deb, she tells me that I will get to eat today. She tells me that I will probably start with something soft – potatoes, pudding, Jell-O . . .

After everything is finished, Robyn brings me to the dining room and we are joined by Myrna, one of Craig's cooks.

"Mark," she tells me, "you get to eat today. I have something special for you."

I never met Myrna, but her easy mannerisms and attention to my particular case just reinforce what a special place Craig is, and how much like a family the staff has become.

Deb carries my tray of food to the table, and I get a huge smile on my face. This is going to be grand. I get to try Lasagna, string beans, mashed potatoes, pudding and a Drink. While I have to take small bites and take my time, I can have all that I want.

I can't quit smiling and take a bite of the potatoes. It's heavenly. That first bite of potatoes is one of the best things I have ever tasted. Mashed potatoes go hand in hand with a country boy's diet. I have now taken another step towards achieving one of the many goals of recovery.

Robyn said that my grin is as big as anything she has ever seen.

Deb asks if I am ok.

I'm overwhelmed, grinning from ear to ear, and really in no position to talk, so I just nod my head vigorously. Which is actually a nod of my entire body.

I take a small bite of the lasagna . . . a small bite of beans . . . another bite of potatoes . . . a spoonful of pudding . . . a small drink – I eat everything on the tray.

So much for not being able to eat much; this was the best meal I'd ever tasted.

Following lunch and the usual round of therapy, Zedo and his girlfriend Corliss come to visit and go to dinner with Robyn and me. Zedo walks with me to the cafeteria, and we all sit down. I order my food and it is brought to my seat.

Robyn, dad and Corliss all order something and bring their trays to the table. They sit down, and Zedo looks at me and says, "I've been waiting three weeks for this . . . I'm so proud of you". Having your father tell you that he is proud of you for *anything* is a powerful motivator and leaves you with the desire to work even harder.

After dinner, we go back to my room to relax, catch up on things at home, and go over my progress in therapy. Now that I can eat, am free of the tubes, staples and wires, it almost feels normal.

The next days and weeks are filled with much of the same therapy sessions. However, now that the trach and the feeding tube have been removed, and the trach incision has closed, I can look forward to starting pool therapy.

Friday, August 27

GOOD EVENING TO all of those of you who are reading and posting ideas on the website.

Today was one of the most wonderful days I have ever had - it ranks right up there with getting married to the best woman ever, finding out she was pregnant and receiving the manager of the year award from CSC about 20 years ago. Why was it such a great day you may be asking yourself - well, it was a great day because we skipped the applesauce entree and went straight to an entire meal. I had lasagna, chopped beans, a banana, mashed potatoes and gravy and a small piece of bread for lunch. And let me tell you that food, albeit from a hospital cafeteria, was the best meal I have ever had. Then to follow it up with dinner and a milkshake snack, it couldn't have been better.

But wait - there is more, we were cleared for a day pass to use anytime this weekend . . . so we are going to go home and just hang out on Sunday.

While Robyn and I were sitting down for dinner, we figured out that it had been 46 days since my last meal . . . ouch! Then we waited for my dad to join us for supper, and we figured out that it had been over 2 months, since he and I had a meal together, and once he did sit down and we started, he made the comment that had has been waiting 3 weeks to have a meal with me . . . what a wonderful feeling.

I hope you all are doing well and thank you for taking the time to write your thoughtful comments and the prayers.

I love you all and look forward to seeing each of you in the near future.

Saturday, August 28

*I*T'S TIME FOR the daily update that I am thrilled to write. Nothing overwhelming or extraordinary today, but I did get my hair cut, ate 3 solid meals, had plenty of visitors and read some great postings - thank you all.

As most of you have seen in the other postings, we got a day pass for tomorrow and I am going to use it to go home and just hang out - play with the dogs, watch my own tv, sit on my own couch, eat our own food, etc.

Next week will be another challenging and successful week and I look forward to sending the update. As I told the Dr's on Thursday, the best is yet to come.

Everyone be safe

love you - Mark

Sunday, August 29

WHAT ANOTHER OUTSTANDING day - I got to go home for the day, where I sat on the couch, watched my own tv, pet my dogs endlessly and ate that turkey sandwich - or what was a resemblance of such - although I didn't eat a complete sandwich, my wonderful sister-in-law picked up lunch for us from the local sandwich shop and Robyn cut the thing into small pieces for me to eat and it was good. The turkey, avocado, tomato, lettuce and small pieces of bread - and yes, I had powerade to wash it all down. And right now, I'm sitting in my hospital bed eating a chocolate shake . . . like I said, what a wonderful day!

I actually look forward to this week to find out what the therapists have planned.

Each day is a challenge, but I am so fortunate to have a great family, wonderful/loving wife and outstanding friends whose positive words and comments never end.

I look forward to sharing tomorrow's moments and about the continued progress.

Love you all
Mark

Week 3

Craig Hospital

Monday, August 30

I AM EATING all three meals every day and having my shake at night. I am consuming over 2000 calories every day as required for the IV to be taken off. The dietician is very pleased with my progress and advises the nurses that she is going to discontinue the tube feeding. Yippee! No more tubes.

I am now gaining some strength back and even though I can use the walker now, I still have to have a therapist, tech or Robyn walk with me. This is still a big improvement; I hate having to have someone push me around the hospital instead of being able to walk myself.

When I arrive at the pool therapy room the first time, I meet Kim, one of the pool therapists. I'm not sure what to expect in pool therapy, and I'm a little anxious to find out what it's all about. Kim helps me do some exercises to stretch my back muscles, work the shoulder muscles and slowly raise my heart rate. The session is 50 minutes long and Holly returns to take me back to my room. I am very tired, but love the fact that I got to do some exercise.

I am going to have pool therapy twice a week to help

loosen up my muscles. Stacey's physical therapy sessions have already made a big difference, and the pool therapy feels like it is only going to speed up my recovery. I am starting to notice that I am able to get around better and feel like I am gaining some strength.

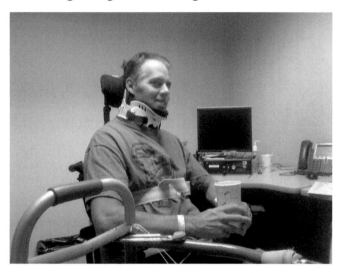

Monday, August 30

ANOTHER WONDERFUL DAY - spent a lot of time in therapy sessions - some of which I don't mind, and some of which are just annoying, but I got to do some stretching and strength movements, which I did enjoy.

Tomorrow is another busy day, but I look forward to it. I continue to eat the scheduled meals and was taken off the last feeding tube today, but am on a calorie count to make sure that I am getting enough calories thru the served meals. I think with the food I am eating and the shakes, I will be good.

Had another neck x-ray today and will review with the Dr tomorrow. Hopefully everything is healing well and we can set a date to get rid of this neck collar - very uncomfortable and annoying.

Still not sleeping well at night, but the Dr told me that starting tonight, they are changing up my med's to hopefully help me sleep thru the night. I think part of the problem had to do with the feeding tube and my need to pee every 2 hours - whichever, tonight we will see.

I want everyone to know how fortunate I am to have such a wonderful wife. She is here at the hospital with me every day first thing in the morning and doesn't leave until just before I am ready to call it a night. I am truly the luckiest person on earth for many reasons.

Keep the positive thoughts coming.

Love you all

Mark

Tuesday, August 31

TODAY WAS ANOTHER great day - spent some time lifting weights and working on stretching . . . unbelievable how much strength I have lost in the last couple of months.

The next few days are filled with more physical therapy and hopefully more physical strength.

Got a pass to go with Robyn to her baby Dr appointment this Tuesday and am excited about it.

Friday I am going to get out in the neighborhood and work on endurance and stamina. We are going to go by the first hospital - St. Anthony's and hopefully see some of those wonderful people who kept me alive.

I went thru the log that Robyn kept during my time at St. Anthony's and am amazed at a lot of things - mostly the medical challenges that took place and the great things the medical teams did to keep me going.

I continue to thank you all for the thoughtfulness and positive words.

Talk to you all soon.

Mark

Wednesday, September 1

MY BROTHER CHRIS visits for the day and walks me to pool therapy. He says that I seem to completely relax when I get into the pool. Today, Kim isn't the therapist; my new one, Sharon, is a huge University of Florida fan, and we hit it right off. The University of Florida is one of my business clients and we talk about Gators football. The conversation quickly expands to college football and my job.

After therapy, Chris walks with me back to my room to change and we have lunch together in the cafeteria. I really like it when someone gets to stay with me . . . especially our family. I have told Robyn that I wish her family were closer so they could visit. As it stands, only Brenda is able to come by when she is not busy, which both Robyn and I appreciate.

For the afternoon PT session, Stacey takes me to the parallel exercise bars and wants to test my balance and strength. She has me hold on to the bars and squat down. I am able to squat a little bit, but it becomes obvious very quickly how weak I have become. Stacey then asks me to stand on one leg. She wants to check my balance. I am able to stand on one leg at a time, but it is evident that there are equilibrium challenges. Between the brain and muscle injuries, I need to work on my balance.

Stacey helps me back to my room and I lie down to relax. Good thing it's almost time for dinner as I am famished.

Wednesday, September 1

THE DAYS KEEP moving forward and remain a challenge - but a good challenge. I lifted weights again today . . . mostly leg and hip exercises, but exercise nonetheless.

We get a day pass to go home on Sunday and Monday in addition to our Friday outing - very excited about that.

I was told by one of the therapists today that I have become a challenge for her daily. She told us today that every night when she goes home, she has to think of new things to test me on because I have exceeded her expectations for the day - that is encouraging news.

Saw the eye Dr today because I had blurry and double vision in the last days at St Anthony's, but he said that my vision and eye muscles are in great shape - more good news and one other thing off the list.

I am going to keep thanking all of the Dr.'s and therapists at Craig, as they are the ones who are going to get me home. I am going to thank each of the Dr.'s and Nurses at St Anthony's, as they are the ones who kept me ticking. The medical profession is a wonderful and thankless profession that doesn't get enough recognition.

Everyone stay safe and I love you all.

Mark

Thursday, September 2

MORE TESTING AT every session: Dr. Berry, Jeanine and Deb have a good baseline from the testing to work with me on cognitive and acuity functions. They continue to give tests to work on memory recall, thought processing and problem solving.

Dr. Weintraub tells me that I can start going home on the weekends, but have to be back at night to take my medication and be observed. Further, I will have to do some additional exercises with Stacey before Robyn can take me anywhere. Just to be sure that it's safe.

That afternoon, Stacey asks Robyn where she has parked. Our Tahoe was in the parking garage across the street. Stacey wants to practice getting in and out of the truck.

We go down the elevator and walk across the street. Standing in front of our truck, Stacey tells me how to get in the seat . . . sit down first, use the seat handle to stabilize myself and keep from falling, then swing my legs and feet in. She's quite insistent that I remember the seatbelt as well.

I go through each step and have no problem . . .yeah! Now we can leave the hospital when allowed.

Stacey tells Robyn to go ahead and drive around the block. She starts to pull out of the parking spot, and Stacey stops us. I roll down my window, and Stacey says, "You have to come back!"

I laugh as my dad has been teasing the nurses and therapists, saying that he is going to take me to Hooters. After reassuring Stacey that I will return, we head off for a quick ride around the Craig campus. We are now out of the shadow of doctors, nurses, hospital workers and other patients and I finally get to enjoy a bit of freedom and normalcy.

When we get back, Robyn gets out of the truck and walks to my side. I open the door and begin to get out. Stop – I have to wait until Robyn puts on the gait belt before we can move any further.

Once everything is in place, Robyn, Stacey and I all walk back to my room. Stacey tells us that things looked good and she will sign my chart to allow me to leave with Robyn.

I keep telling Stacey that I want to do more, and she continues to maintain that a gradual integration of activity is a better way to go. I keep bugging Stacey, so she takes me to the exercise bike. She tells me that I can ride the bike anytime, but there has to be a therapist in the room who is aware that I am on the bike.

I get on the bike and Stacey tells me to start pedaling. She tells me that I am going to pedal for 10 minutes at level five. I begin to pedal and quickly discover that this is too much, so Stacey reduces it to level three.

I keep pedaling. After three minutes, I am already tired and stop pedaling to take a break. Invariably, Stacey asks if me if I am ok, and tells me that I can stop if I would like to. Stubborn to the end, I refuse to give up and start pedaling again. After another three minutes, I need another break. Another few minutes go by, and once again, I need a break . . . 3 breaks in 10 minutes. I am so disappointed in myself and what I have become, I tell myself that I will never allow my body to get to the same point again. My mind races back to the image of that person in the mirror. Somehow, it feels like I could have done something differently and prevented this slide into infirmity. I am surprised to discover that I feel guilty!

Stacey has probably dealt with this before and asks, "What are your goals?"

After seeing how much my physical abilities had degraded, I set my goal of time to be twice what I was expected to reach upon the first challenge. I had been an athlete all my life – always seeking to overachieve when told I couldn't do something; something in me was driven to beat challenges, and some of this fire is starting to come back to me. "By the time I leave this hospital, I want to be doing twenty minutes at level five."

"That's admirable," she says, "but don't push it."

"I'll do it safely, but I am going to push it. I need to get there."

The Next Step

Friday, September 3

THINGS ARE BECOMING routine and I am starting to fully understand the severity of my brain injury. I understand the intent of all my therapy sessions, and I am beginning to recognize the positive changes and recovery of my injury. I see all my cognitive functions getting better – my deductive reasoning is improving, my frustration is diminishing, and I understand what I need to complete so I can go home.

Since I have been cleared to take outings with Robyn, we have been allowed a pass for the afternoon to go anywhere we want. I tell Robyn that I want to go back to St Anthony's hospital to visit everyone who was part of the medical team that saved my life.

Earlier that morning, I was informed that my 3-day calorie count averaged over 2600 calories, so there is no longer a concern that I am not going to get enough nutrients.

After lunch, I meet Robyn at my room and get ready to take the outing. We get in the truck and start driving to the hospital. Along the way, I tell Robyn that I want to call Damon. He is surprised to hear from me, as this is the first time I have gotten to really talk to him since the accident. We speak for a few minutes, and I tell Damon about all the therapy sessions I have to go through and about the different therapists. Damon tells me about his pair of visits to the hospital, and how the first one was a little emotional as he was saying his good-byes. He tells me that when he was in the hospital room with Robyn, he worried that he was going to have to wait another year to be an uncle. He had long hoped that Robyn and I might start a family soon.

You may recall that during his first visit, as he was leaving, he and Robyn had an emotional good-bye, and Robyn told Damon that she was pregnant. When he returned for his second visit, I was trying to explain the happy news about our child with gestures and signs. He hadn't wanted to spoil my fun by telling me that he knew and had simply played along.

When I hang up the phone, I turn towards Robyn and say, "You sold out? I thought you didn't tell anyone yet?"

"I couldn't help it. We were in your room together, and he was getting ready to leave. I was crying, he was crying, and then he made the comment about waiting a year . . . I couldn't hold it – I had to tell him. I couldn't let him leave like that."

When we get to St. Anthony's and park, I have to wait for Robyn to help me out of the truck before we start walking, but I don't mind because I finally get to walk outside in a place away from Craig . . . back into the public mainstream.

We walk in together, and Robyn sees the hospital patient advocate who was instrumental in helping her understand our options and in getting us to Craig Hospital. The two of them talk as old acquaintances do, but I am at a bit of a loss. Even though I had seen her, I simply cannot remember anything about her.

We go up the elevator to the 2nd floor – the Neurological Surgery Intensive Care Unit, or NSICU. As we walk in, the room conjures an eerie feeling . . . I spent over a month in this place and don't remember anything. The ICU is a large room with the nurses' station in the center. The medical teams can sit in this area to review charts, talk amongst themselves and see all the patients. Robyn points out room 210, the room where I spent most of my time, and to a few of the nurses that she remembers.

The first nurse, Sherry, comes up and is shocked to see me . . . here I was – walking back into the place that kept me alive. Tears quickly began to flow from her and Robyn, and I am very appreciative. I tell Sherry thank you, give her a hug and apologize for not remembering her. Sherry asks how we all are doing and asks about Zedo. Apparently, she and Zedo shared quite a few laughs.

Sherry has to go back to work, so Robyn shows me the waiting room that she, Zedo, Nancy, Bonnie, Gerald, all our family and friends shared for so many days and nights. It is a very quiet and somber place. But while we were there, I see an old coworker named Ron. He was waiting with a friend of his whose daughter was severely injured in a car accident the night before. They tell me that she is stable, but struggling like all patients in that part of the hospital.

After the short visit with Ron, we go back into the ICU, and see another nurse, Jane, who looked after us. She embraces us like lost family when we walk through the door.

Finally, a third nurse who attended to me quite frequently, Matt, had just come on duty. He too spends a few minutes talking to us.

When the visits to the NSICU were done, Robyn walks us down the hall to the room where I spent my last couple nights. The nurses there weren't as familiar, but they remember our stay.

On the way back to the elevator, I notice a doctor walking towards us.

I ask Robyn, "Is that one of my doctors?"

"It is. He did your neck surgery - Dr. Henderhiser."

"I remember him. He came to my room and talked about doing a surgery."

As we get closer, Dr. Henderhiser recognizes us too.

I say hello and put my hand out.

Dr. Henderhiser has a soft drink in one hand and a bag of chips in the other, so he has to do a quick adjustment.

As he does, I say, "I remember you. You were in my room one day holding the same thing . . . a Coke in one hand and a bag of Sun Chips in the other".

"Yeah . . . the diet of a doctor. How are you?"

"I'm doing well – I really appreciate everything you did for me . . . for us"

In the time since, Dr. Henderhiser has become a close friend of ours and is a wonderful person first and fantastic doctor second.

We slowly walk back to the truck and headed back to Craig . . . I was tired and needed to lie down.

While we were in the truck, Robyn asks if I was ok.

"I'm fine. It was weird to go back to a place and see people I had met, but didn't remember."

Robyn points out an open space between the hospital and hospital chapel, and tells me about an afternoon when she was so tired, that she needed to rest. So she and Dixie walked down to the grass, laid down and stared into the sky. They both fell asleep, while Bonnie made sure nobody disturbed them. This had been a moment of tranquility for Robyn. Being able to lay back and not think about anything. Not having to answer questions about how I was doing or what was next. Having the comfort of her mother watching over her again.

Friday, September 3

WHAT AN OUTSTANDING and humbling day. As I wrote in the past couple of entries, I was a little nervous going back to St Anthony's, but we made the trip today and it was a little emotional. I mean going back to the place where the fine medical staff grabbed me from the clutches of death and brought me back to life and to the place I am now. I was able to see 2 of the great Nurses in the ICU and the Dr who did the surgery on my neck. Both of the Nurses cried and I have to tell you that I shed a tear myself. They were so amazed at my being able to walk in and were grateful that I would spend my day saying hello and thanking them.

The rest of the day went just as well in a different way. I went to Robyn's school and spent some time visiting with her colleagues and some of her students before going back to the hospital.

The afternoon sessions of therapy included doing some squats, hamstring extensions and hand-eye exercises. Then I went into the memory therapist and did some number exercises that I kicked-ass on.

I finished with more physical therapy that included more

stretching and work on my shoulder and spine.

Tomorrow is a day off with visitors, but I think I will still get on the exercise bike and work on my stamina. I was also cleared to be "independent" today, which means I don't have to have anyone with me to move within my room, walk the hospital halls or go to the cafeteria . . . One more step to getting out of here.

We are taking advantage of the day pass and going home on Sunday and Monday and will enjoy every moment of it.

I am always so thrilled to read the great comments that each of you post and appreciate your taking the time.

Have a great weekend and fine Labor Day and will update again tomorrow.

Mark

Saturday, September 4

*A*LTHOUGH THINGS WERE *quiet around the hospital, we tried to keep things moving. I spent some time on the exercise bike; Robyn and I went to get lunch; and we had several visitors. Tomorrow will bring more down time, but it will be at home relaxing and hanging with the dogs.*

Next week will bring more challenges, but the more, the better. I plan on knocking down each task the therapists present and give them good reason to consider giving me an earlier discharge date.

The other great thing about today was the official start of college football season. The only unfortunate thing is that I am not at a game somewhere . . . but the bright side of that is I get to be home with my wife and friends. The days would be long and less fulfilling without having the love of my life by my side. I am truly the luckiest man in the world for many reasons.

I continue to think of each of you and hope that everyone is doing well. Stay positive and don't take advantage of anything during your day. Look at each thing as a benefit and in a positive light . . . things may not make sense at the time, but they don't have to . . . you just need to live each day to its fullest.

Thank you all again for the entries, the comments and positive thoughts.

The weekend is something special. I go home Saturday, Sunday and Monday (since Monday was a holiday), however I have to return to Craig each night. We have several visitors while home. On Monday we enjoy a meeting with Todd and Janet for a late breakfast before going home to enjoy some quiet time on our own couch.

The week picks right up where Friday left us: achieving higher goals for myself on the bike and in physical therapy. However, Tuesday is extra special, as I go with Robyn to her first baby doctor appointment. I hear the baby's heartbeat with the ultrasound and see the little one dancing around in her belly with both arms and legs flailing . . . it's cool!

Week 4
Craig Hospital

Wednesday, September 8

I SEEM TO BE moving along quite well, and my brother Chris comes to spend the day with me. He brings my nephews Chase and Bryce along as well. One of the therapy sessions is time in the pool, and Chris, Chase and Bryce all get in with me. We play some volleyball with another patient, and we all really enjoy the time.

The Craig approach to therapy involves having a social life in order to create the sense that nothing has changed with you personally. They invite and ask for family to be included in every step of the rehabilitation process, so during my pool sessions, both Kim and Sharon suggest that I invite family to the therapy sessions in the pool. Having a piece of your life with family highlights how important their roles are in the therapy and rehabilitation process. By having open arms and minds for the patient needs and their families, Craig allows for a level of comfort for those experiencing a difficult transition.

Wednesday, September 8

ANOTHER FORWARD MOVING day - spent time in the therapy pool (95 degrees and awesome) - primarily working on range of motion with my shoulders and strengthening, then on to the physical therapist, which was a butt kicker today. She put a whuppin' on me. My back is out of alignment because of the rib fractures and she is doing some physical adjusting to get me back where I should be - a little sore tonight. Then I spent time with the speech therapist and clinical psychologist - both good people who I really like.

My brother Chris was here all day with me, which I enjoy. He went to all the therapy sessions with me and actually got in the therapy pool while I was in there.

I'm going to the grocery store tomorrow with the occupational therapist and picking up food to make dinner for Robyn and me on Friday. Making baked chicken, pasta, meat sauce, carrots and pudding. They won't let me grill yet, but I'm excited that I get to make us a meal.

Spent more time on the exercise bike today - upped the time to 14 minutes and finished the last minute at an increased resistance level. The physical therapist asked me today where I wanted to be when I reached the discharge date and I told her that I want to ride 20 minutes at level 5. She said that they would be happy with that, but I then asked her if I need to do more time or an increased resistance level and she said that my goal was appropriate.

I was also told by the Dr today that they are ready for me to move to the next step, which is moving into an on-site apartment that has a kitchenette, couch and a shower. So by the middle or end of next week, I will be moving into the new pad.

We are going to get to go home again on Saturday and Sunday, which I always look forward to.

Keep the positive thoughts coming and cherish each moment - forget about the things that get under your skin, because they are just things.

Look forward to seeing everyone soon.
Mark

Thursday, September 9

ANOTHER POSITIVE DAY, but I am ready to get out of here. The next 3 weeks will bring some challenges, and I welcome every one of them, but I am still ready to go home.

Today started early with my meeting with one of the occupational therapists and going to Safeway for tomorrow night's dinner. She asked if I wanted to take the bus . . . but hey - how am I going to get stronger if I don't take advantage of all the exercise possible, so we walked the 5 blocks and walked back.

Today, more muscle manipulation and a leg workout, followed by more time on the bike.

Had friends come by to visit, which is always nice. Tomorrow is Smashburger time with one of the Nurses, since I promised her a cheeseburger when she got back from vacation. It will be awesome! Janet - you will get a detailed description of the burger and how I savored every bite.

I do get to go home again for the weekend, and the only downside to that is that I have to come back at night.

Only 3 more weeks!

I can tell you that the next time I hear someone complain

about their day or something that happened during their day, I am going to invite them for a visit to Craig Hospital. There are some extremely determined people at this place whose abilities have been restricted due to an unfortunate accident, and they keep on pushing forward. Something we all need to do . . . push forward regardless of the daily hurdles.

I will update you tomorrow about the burger and the chicken and pasta dinner.

Everyone be safe and I can never thank each of you enough for the kind thoughts and comments. It is pretty overwhelming to log in each day and see that almost 14k of you have accessed the site to read the updates or others comments - it is a real moral and attitude boost.

Talk to all of you soon and be safe.

Mark

What a great weekend. I had promised Bert, my nurse, that when she returned from vacation, she and I would have a cheeseburger together. When Bert had left for vacation, I wasn't eating solid foods, and now that she was back, it is time to share a meal.

Part of moving toward independence includes demonstrating that I can take care of myself in the kitchen. Therefore, I get to cook dinner for Robyn. I make extra so my dad and Corliss can join us for baked chicken over pasta with peas and pudding.

Then to top off the day, my Aunt Diane, Uncle Eldon and Cousin Alex come by tonight and bring me four dozen Chocolate Chip cookies - yum! Maybe these will help me put some weight back on.

Sunday is another amazing day. Church is truly a remarkable experience. Many of the members of St. Peter's Lutheran church have been following our progress since the accident and many visited while I was at St Anthony's. Each and every one of them is welcoming and had great words to share when we arrive.

As much as I appreciate all their thoughts and prayers, I have to share a story about a young man who we got to meet today. After we arrive at church and find our place to sit down, we sit in front of this family whom we have never met. They are a wonderful family with three young kids, with the oldest about seven. When it was time to share God's peace among the congregation, we turned and saw this family. Mom is almost in tears and explains that her oldest son, Payton, has been praying for my recovery since the day the congregation was told about our accident. He had told his mom that he didn't know who I was, but he was going to pray for me every day. So when we came in and sat down in front of them, Payton's mom told him who I was, and he was so proud. Tell me that doesn't bring a tear to your eye. God bless Payton and all those who have included me in their prayers.

Week 5

Craig Hospital

Monday, September 13

WHAT A TRULY outstanding day. I found out that I am making the next move in therapy and moving into the apartment on Wednesday. But better than that, I was told today that my new discharge date is September 23rd - a week earlier than first scheduled. It goes to show that hard work, perseverance and following the Dr's plan works - and of course the prayers and positive thoughts provide the intangible support.

There will be plenty of work to do once I am discharged. I will have to return for out-patient therapy for a few months, but being home will be a huge therapeutic step.

Other than that, I continue to push hard on the bike and in all therapy sessions to make myself as good as I can be on discharge date.

I don't know how I can thank all of you enough. In addition to all the time each of you have spent reading the updates, writing your thoughts and for the phone calls and personal visits. The human spirit is truly a remarkable thing and I will never forget any of you. If there is anything I can do for anyone, please do not hesitate to let me know. I may *not be able to jump in and help with physical labor for a few months, but I will be happy to assist with anything else.*

Kate - you have a wonderful young man in Payton and please let him know that I look forward to seeing him again.

See you all soon.

Mark

Tuesday, September 14

ANOTHER PROGRESSIVE DAY and I can't wait to see what tomorrow and the future bring . . .I am ready for any challenge that the therapists or Dr's want to give . . .nothing is going to stop me from moving forward and taking care of my family again. In the grand scheme of things, nothing is as important as my family. When I get out of here, I am going to do everything in my power to make sure I do whatever I can for them and those in need.

Today I had to find a statement in a book and write a paragraph of what my thoughts were. I chose to write about what I would want every year for my birthday if it was affordable. I wrote that I wish that everyone would take a step back and do something nice for a complete stranger.

The human spirit is strong and a few positive words of encouragement go a long way.

I will forever be grateful to all of you for writing and the positive thoughts . . . but do the same for anyone in need - you will make their day!

When I write tomorrow, I will be in my own "apartment" getting ready for those final 7 days . . . which is really only 5

213

days since we get to go home again for the weekend.

I ask that you all hug and tell those you care about how much you love them . . . you can never share those thoughts enough.

Love you all and see to you soon.

Mark

Wednesday, September 15

MOVED INTO THE new pad today and it is truly an apartment. The best thing about it is having my own bathroom shower and a double bed.

Our friends Krischel and Sean brought us B-B-Q dinner tonight and my dad and Corliss were able to stay and have a great impromptu dinner party . . . what great friends and family we have.

Many of you have written expressing your thoughts about what family can do to support us. And I can easily say that the family has been a huge inspiration for me. Robyn is a star - spending each day with me, helping whenever and wherever possible and lately going to work all day and coming directly to the hospital afterward, while nurturing our baby to be. My dad, mother, brother, sister, nieces, nephews, aunts, uncles, cousins, Corliss and all the other family that I may have missed have been by my side from the beginning and have kept a positive attitude since day one. I can't thank my in-laws enough for their support and dropping whatever they had going on to help Robyn and the rest of us whenever they could. Nobody could ask for a better family. Then there is my second family - everyone at CSC. It has been truly remarkable and a bit emotional at times reading their messages and speaking with them. And of course - not last and certainly not least - my friends. We have the most awesome group of friends who are thoughtful, considerate and truly care about us. So you ask why I am inspired - that is where I get my inspiration and spirit.

Tomorrow we get to go to Home Depot to pick up some things for the house for my arrival next week - I still can't totally believe that they are letting me go a week early, but I am going to continue to work hard to prove that they made the right decision and set the bar for the next patient who can challenge each therapist and define themselves.

We get to go home again for the weekend and I always look forward to that time. We don't do much while we are home, which is just as well. We get to relax in our own shell and truly enjoy the time off . . . soon enough it will be permanent.

I know I keep saying it, but I truly appreciate all of you taking the time to read the journal and write your own thoughts. I look forward to seeing you all again in the near future and keep up the positive attitude.

Mark

Thursday, September 16

*T*ODAY WAS A *good day, but I am ready to go home . . . only 6 more days and the second part of the recovery begins. As much as the apartment is nice, it's not home. I did get to sleep in a double bed that didn't have a raised back, which resulted in the best night sleep I have had since I've been here - that and additional anti-inflammatory medication that helped relieve some of the back and shoulder pain I have been experiencing.*

Had a good day in therapy. Took 2 of the therapists with Robyn and me to Home Depot and picked up a couple of things in preparation for being home.

Spent more time in the therapy pool - which is awesome; think about climbing into a 95 degree pool and working on stretching - hard to describe and understand, but believe me when I say that it is better than a hot tub.

Had 2 sessions with the Physical Therapist who worked on stretching all my tight and out of place back muscles, and then I sucked it up thru the "Power Hour" workout.

Spent more time on the bike and have increased the resistance another level towards my goal.

Had a session with the Clinical Psychologist and talked about moving back into the work mode, which he understood and actually agreed with my idea to slowly slide back into it.

One of the therapists actually told me I was a miracle for working thru the recovery so fast, which made me feel good about my efforts and their confidence.

Tomorrow should be another typical day that I will attack with all my effort and attitude. The weekend will be awesome at home, and I look forward to next Thursday.

I cherish each and every thought that you have shared and look forward to seeing each and every one of you.

Be Safe and love you all.

Mark

Friday, September 17

ONLY 4 MORE days at the hospital! Yeah! Going home tomorrow and Sunday and will enjoy every moment of it. My good friend (and family member), Stephen is going to join me tomorrow to watch football and share some laughs.

Went out to dinner with our other good friends Todd and Janet tonight and always enjoy their company.

I am so fortunate to have all of you as my friends and can never express my gratitude enough for your caring and taking the time to visit the website and write your words.

Today was another normal rehab day - work on memory games, do some stretching, some light lifting and spending time with the therapists.

Had a bit of interesting news today from my Dr. As you may recall from a prior posting, I have had some difficulty with my left shoulder as it pertains to strength and discomfort. My Dr suggested that there may be an impingement that is going to require an MRI and nerve test. He believes that I may have torn something in my shoulder which would require some kind of surgery. This can also have something to do with the fracture of my C-7 vertebrae, which would have an impact with the nerve connection thru the shoulder, thru my forearm and into my hand. We will know more next week - but it has no effect on my brain injury or my ability to function, so I am happy about that.

The new room as been wonderful in many ways. The most beneficial in my opinion has to do with having a double bed. I can now spread out a little bit and have been sleeping somewhat on my side, which has resulted in 2 of the best night sleep since I arrived here a month ago.

I won't be back on until Monday night since another weekend is here, but I hope you all have a safe and enjoyable couple of days.

Talk to you soon.

Mark

Week 6

Craig Hospital

Monday, September 20

REMEMBER THAT EMG test that needed to be scheduled? Well it's today. So Dustin from transport comes in and loads me into a wheelchair. We go to the neurosciences lab at Swedish Hospital, and wait for the doctor.

The EMG test consists of having electrical wires hooked up to various parts of your body, and then holding onto another electrical pad in the palm of your hand. Then the doctor has the machine send electrical current into one wire and measures the time it takes the current to travel to the other end. This will determine if there is nerve damage, and if so, where it might be located.

The first testing is done and nothing 'bright,' as they call it, is noticed.

The second stage of tests consists of having a needle stuck into various places of the arm, wrist and hand, and again, having electrical current shot through the circuit.

The second one is uncomfortable, to put it lightly. This testing goes on for about ten minutes and I start getting agitated. The results note that there is some damage, which is probably from the C7 vertebrae injury, but nothing serious enough to require surgery.

I return to my room not happy.

Monday, September 20

3 NIGHTS AND 4 days . . .aaahhh! I can see the end of this tunnel. Had a nerve test done on my left arm and hand today - Holy Crap! That was uncomfortable - nothing like having electrodes attached to different places on your hand and fingers and having shock sent thru your arm. I will never do that again, but the test showed positive "conductivity" thru my nerves in my arm to my hand, so the numbness and pain that I have been experiencing is reduced to something in my shoulder . . . which could have something to do with the limited strength and range of motion. I'm going to guess that the shoulder x-ray and MRI is next to see what else could be the problem. But these little hurdles are nothing in the grand scheme of things . . . just something else to face and defeat.

Going home is going to be great and I know that the rest of my recovery will accelerate when I am in my own environment, but at the same time it's going to be a little difficult. Why you ask? Well, because I am going to be limited as to what I can do . . . no yard work, no Driving to the gym or store, no working on the house, etc. Those are things that I like to do and won't be able to just handle. But in due time, it will all be back.

I know I have said it before, and I am sure that you have heard it from other people in your life, but Cherish each and every moment of every day. I was telling a friend of mine today during a different conversation, that the lives of Robyn and I were changed in 58 feet and a matter of 3 seconds. In some ways I think I am going to be a better person, but I would never want to go thru the same thing again as what we have been thru this past 9 weeks.

You are all wonderful people and I want the best for each and every one of you. Don't forget to live your lives the best you know how and you will always have the support and love from those around you . . . you certainly will always have mine.

Have a great week as I know I will, and I look forward to writing again tomorrow.

Mark

Tuesday, September 21

*A*NOTHER DAY DONE *and one more step closer to the finish line. Things are pretty status-quo right now. Physical fitness training to include stretching and working on my back. More tests to evaluate my brain recovery . . . a lot of the same tests that I took when I got here 5 weeks ago. This is a little annoying but gratifying at the same time. It is interesting and encouraging to see where I was when I arrived and where I am now. The funny thing is, some of the tests seem so easy now and to see what I didn't complete or what I was confused on before really puts into perspective the degree of my brain injury.*

We have the meeting with the Dr, therapists, and the family tomorrow to discuss what I need to do for my future and where I have had improvements. I am also going to ask to see my chart starting with the day that I arrived. I want to see what the progress was medically and what everyone's interpretation was when I first arrived. I'm sure the general consensus will be that I was angry and outspoken about my being here . . . which I admit. When I got to Craig hospital, I didn't want to be here and didn't think that I should be here.

Thankfully I had Robyn, my dad, and patient Nurses who showed me why it was necessary to listen to the doctors and therapists and be patient with their program. I tell you, it has paid off. I am not only better medically, but I believe I am a better person because of it.

During my posts in the past 5 weeks, I have shared personal thoughts about what we can do personally to live our lives better. These thoughts are only my opinions and what I feel is good practice. In the end, you have to live your lives the best way you see fit. I want everyone to be safe with what you do. I look forward to seeing everyone and keep the positive attitudes.

Love you all.

Mark

Wednesday, September 22

*D*OWN TO MY last night - had a pretty productive day overall. The physical therapist continues to work on my back to get me straightened out (she can put a hurtin' on me in very little time, but I know it is a good hurt). We had our discharge meeting with the Dr and therapists and the general theme of my being home is to be smart and careful . . . that, and Robyn is the boss.

I will be able to start working myself into light work in the coming weeks, but certainly will have to gauge the level of involvement based on my energy level. The Dr was very clear that I had a severe brain injury and there is still a long road to go before I reach full-recovery . . . which I will achieve.

The out-patient schedule is a little daunting next week as I have to be at Craig Hospital 4 days and incorporate an appointment with the neck surgeon, the ear/nose/throat Dr to check my vocal chords, the removal of my stomach tube, and another MRI on my neck. Yes, it will be busy, but it is just another step in the road to recovery.

Had my MRI on the shoulder tonight and will be able to review the results with the Dr next Wednesday. The EMG test that was conducted on Monday came back positive, so there is no permanent nerve damage in my arm, but the MRI on my shoulder and neck will help pinpoint what is going on with my hand and finger numbness. Whatever is found will be nothing compared to what we have gone thru this past 9 weeks.

I can't tell you how fortunate I have been to have the family support, friend support, your support and certainly the medical support. Without any one of them, I wouldn't be as successful as I am right now.

Although I am leaving the hospital tomorrow, I will keep the updates coming on Caring Bridge for now. I will figure out a way to keep in touch with all of you post Caring Bridge at another date.

I wish everyone the best and be safe.

Love you all

Mark

September 23, 2010

NOT ONLY IS today my birthday, but after spending almost ten weeks in a hospital, I finally get to go home. The day isn't without challenges though. Before I can be discharged, I have to have the upper GI feeding tube removed from my stomach. Much like the nasal tube, this one is a bit painful. The Doctor cuts the sutures and begins unwinding the tube from itself while still in my stomach. I would equate this to being punched in the gut over and over. When it is finally removed, the relief is far from instant. This tube had been in my stomach for five weeks now, and had become part of my body. The trauma of removal causes me to experience cramps and shooting pain throughout my entire stomach area. Because of this pain and discomfort, the doctors will not release me until they are convinced that there is no abdominal or intestinal damage. So, back to the X-ray department to have a complete upper GI X-Ray, which consists of lying on my side (not easy with the neck collar still on) and drinking iodine while the technicians take X-rays. The doctors have to make sure that there is no leakage anywhere in my digestive system.

Regardless, everything comes up clear and Craig finally lets me go home.

The X-ray and exam wasn't painful, but the side effect of drinking that iodine is. I am nauseous for the rest of the day and through the night. At one point around 3:00 am, I almost wake Robyn up to take me back to the hospital. But I suck it up, lie back down and finally fall asleep. When I wake up later in the morning, I finally feel better. I am finally home.

Home Again

The Final Stretch

THE COMING WEEKS and months were going to bring their own set of challenges. I was not allowed to drive, so any appointments or errands required my reaching out to friends for help. Each and every one of them gladly stepped in without hesitation and helped with anything I asked.

I needed to start integrating myself into a daily routine and comfort zone, which meant slowly re-engaging work projects, house projects and preparing for a baby to arrive. But the doctors insisted that I pace myself and get plenty of rest. I took their advice as much as possible and would only work on items until I felt fatigued – mentally or physically; sometimes both. A person can only rest so much, watch the news so many times and throw the ball for the dogs so many times, before a change needs to happen.

I wanted to know more about the accident itself, so I began reading the accident and medical reports. There is a lot of interesting stuff in there . . . scary, but interesting.

We were traveling at about 45 mph when a car turned in front of us. I tried to stop the motorcycle, but there were only 58 feet to stop in . . . not enough. The motorcycle started sliding when Robyn was somehow ejected from her seat, but I was still holding onto the handlebars and slammed into the side of the car, sending me head first into the car. It is believed that for that split second while the bike was sliding and before impact, I reached behind me and pulled Robyn off the bike so she would be safe.

Bystanders called 911 at 12:15 and the paramedics arrived at the scene three minutes later. When they arrived, they stated that the fire department and bystanders had removed the motorcycle from me as I was lying face down under the car. My nose, mouth and ears were bleeding a little, but I would respond incomprehensibly to verbal commands.

The paramedics stabilized me and put me in the ambulance with Robyn, and left for the hospital at 12:29. At 12:34 we arrived at Heart of the Rockies Medical Center in Salida and immediately received treatment from the Emergency Room Trauma team.

After having my injuries diagnosed, I was still having problems breathing. So the doctor actually cut a hole into the side of my chest and inserted a tube directly into my lung. He drained about one litre of old black blood from me. After that, I began breathing better.

The medical reports from St Anthony's were numerous and very medical. I took several days to read each one and try to understand every procedure and treatment report .. . *Fascinating stuff*. I now know more than I would ever think is possible about the anatomy of the neck and back, neurological background and traumatic brain injuries. I guess the consistent theme was that I was *LUCKY!*

The first week of Outpatient therapy kicked off full-throttle with 4 sessions and gradually went down to three days, then two days. The first week was a bit frustrating as the entire therapy team, except for Dr. Barry was completely new. I had to describe all of my previous therapies to each of them, revisit old tests and complete some new ones. The repeats allowed my new therapists to gauge their own plan of therapy. And since I incurred a brain injury, both my driver's license and pilot's medical certificate had been suspended. My driver's license would not be reissued until I was able to complete a driving program and evaluation, in addition to the standard test at the DMV. Fortunately, Craig Hospital had a driving program and I quickly enlisted in the class. Regaining my Third Class FAA medical certificate was going to be a much different story and fraught with many challenges.

In the coming weeks and months, I faced multiple doctors' appointments; the first being the one I looked forward to most. This was the follow up appointment with Dr. Henderhiser. After reviewing a cervical x-ray, he suggested that it was possible to begin weaning myself off the neck collar and regaining my mobility. And just like that, we were on track to have the rods and screws removed from the C2 bone sometime in mid to late January.

This was great news! After a long discussion about the trauma and fractures, I still had two looming questions. I asked the Doctor, "If I was your relative, would you do this procedure?"

Without delay and leveling a serious gaze at me, he responded, "absolutely".

My other question was, "What are the chances that I would re-break either the C2 or C7 vertebrae doing everyday things that I was used to doing?"

Again, without hesitation, and looking me directly in the eye, he said, "very unlikely".

"So why is it that this stabilization procedure had never been done before?"

His response was a bit scary: "Usually when a person has a break in the C-2, they die, so there has never been a real need to consider this procedure as an alternative."

Needless to say, I felt a huge relief when we left his office.

Of course, not everything was good news. As you may recall, I'd had a persistent problem with numbness and muscle tightness in my left forearm and hand, which the doctor felt may have had something to do with the displacement of the C7 towards the C6, pinching a nerve. I was told that the only way to truly correct the problem would be to fuse the two vertebrae. The procedure would have little effect on my range of motion, but would require another surgery and another six months in the collar. However, he didn't rule out a problem in the soft-tissue of my shoulder and wanted to see the EEG and shoulder MRI before making a final decision. He also suggested that I could try to continue to strengthen the entire arm muscle group and see how that works,

This would require extra work in physical therapy and personal work at the gym. The physical therapists weren't excited about me doing my own work and wouldn't approve me going to the gym without first writing out my workout routine and having them review it. I wanted to get back to the gym, where I knew how to push my body back to who I was and where I was comfortable. Sitting at home did not offer that opportunity, so I wrote a plan that focused on stretching and light strength training. This meant taking things slow and letting my body dictate the path.

I identified dates and goals to focus on regaining my former, physical self . . . I wanted to be ready to hold that baby.

As the weeks went by, Robyn had multiple appointments with the OBGYN to check on the development of our baby. We spent the intervening time picking out baby furniture, clothes, bedding, accessories and anything baby that we thought was needed. This was getting exciting!

As the days roll by, therapy continued and I was able to take on more work tasks. Finally on November 21, I got to make my first work trip. We did a lot of work with Major League Soccer, and I was invited to Toronto for the MLS Cup game. Robyn traveled with me and we got to see Damon for the first time that I remember. We saw many other friends and business associates which was all very rewarding. Getting back to work helped me to find a new resolve in my recovery process. A few weeks later, Robyn and I traveled to Los Angeles for a football game at the Rose Bowl, which again, was very gratifying.

While all of this was happening and I started getting back into my professional routine, I had continued to work on improving my shoulder strength. However, I wasn't making much progress. So I saw another doctor in Dr. Henderhiser's office - one who specialized in shoulder and knee injuries. The MRI he ordered revealed a tear in my rotator cuff - an injury that would require another surgery.

November 2, 2010

AFTER A LOT of work, I finally got to take my neck collar off on a semi-permanent basis. Although it was for only 2 hours a day, it was a very welcome relief. I got to do things that I was only dreaming about a short time ago. I got to sleep without the collar, which meant that I was able to sleep on my side. Of course, I was a little nervous the first night and didn't sleep well, but the next night felt like I hadn't slept in a month. It took some time to really get readjusted, but time was one thing I had plenty of. Another first was something that we all take for granted: I was able to drink water from the sink by cupping my hands under the faucet. Since I'd had the collar on before, the only way to drink was by using a cup. Now when I brushed my teeth, I could cup my hands, collect water and rinse out my mouth; like I said—the little things.

Nevertheless, having the collar off was a bit trying and nerve racking because I was so used to it. Now I had to be very careful while trying to move my head, but it was necessary to work the muscles. Because I had been immobilized for so long, the muscles and tendons in my neck had stiffened up and it was difficult to rotate from side to side very much. Initially my range of motion to the left was about 15 degrees and my range to the right was about 20 degrees.

I completed my driving test on December 8, taking me closer to full independence. I was finally able to drive myself to the gym, take business trips alone and run errands.

December 15, 2010

I FINALLY HAD my shoulder surgery, which was, thankfully, uneventful. But what followed was another stage of hard work: rehab. Rehab involved many of the same exercises as before but with much more determination. Moreover, baby time was right around the corner and I had to be ready. But just as we thought things were closing in on the last step, we made another small discovery. While I was at the gym in the midst of my workout, I was a little shocked to find blood in my urine. At the time, I believed this might have been be an anomaly – after all, it was painless, so I went home and got ready for the day. But the problem persisted. The next time I needed to urinate, I discovered more blood. This couldn't have been a good sign., so while I was at physical therapy later that day, I mentioned the episode to Celeste, my physical therapist, who took me to the ER for evaluation. They confirmed that there was still blood in my urine and referred me to a urologist.

I saw Dr. Allen, who determined that there were three stones in my bladder left over from my coma and the extended catheter use that entailed.

See, when a catheter is used, part of it is inflated with air to hold the urinary passages open so that fluid can easily flow from the bladder into the catheter. This 'balloon' will usually develop a crystalline coating on it from the constant exposure to urine. When the balloon was deflated and removed, the crystal coating broke apart. Normally, these bits of crystalline urine break down on their own and are passed through the urinary tract. But sometimes, as in my case, pieces will stay in the bladder and need to be surgically removed.

Fortunately, the procedure was mercifully short.

February 17, 2011

THE LAST PIECE that needed to be addressed was the removal of the two metal rods and screws from my neck. Once again, I was in the care of Dr. Henderhiser.

Dr. Henderhiser checked over his notes, and asked, "Are you ready?"

"I am – let's do this . . . did you get a good night's rest last night?"

He chuckled, "I sure did."

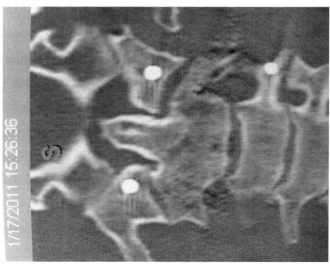

I was given anesthesia through an IV and moved down the hallway to surgery. A couple hours later, I woke up with Robyn standing next to me. We were moved to another room in the hospital, and I got to go home the next morning, and begin the next step of recovery: physical therapy for my neck.

After the three rods and six screws were removed and my rehabilitation routine was established, I needed to set new goals. My first was to be as healthy as possible for our baby. I needed to work on building rotation in my neck, getting rest and delegating as much work as possible. My second goal was to enter and complete the "*Cherry Creek Sneak*" race. The race is a five-mile course for runners thru the Cherry Creek neighborhood of Denver held annually the first weekend in May. While I didn't shatter any time records, I did complete the race. My immediate final goal was to complete a 'Boot Camp' session with one of the trainers at the gym.

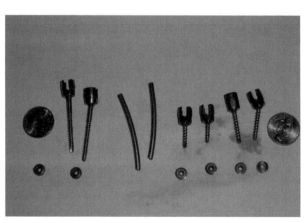

Moving On

SINCE JULY 18TH, things have been a whirlwind, and as you may imagine, completely unpredictable and surprising. As many of you may recall, the first month at St. Anthony's didn't exist in my mind. I had so much medication being pumped into me, that I recall almost nothing. If I had a conversation with someone who came to visit in the last week of my stay there, I could sometimes recall their presence and conversation, but if I had to write about the last week . . . I would not be able to do it.

Thus it was so important and appreciated that Robyn kept a daily journal and maintained the Caring Bridge entries, the emails, cards and personal messages that were being passed around. Even to this day, I like talking to those who visited during my time at Craig and while I was recovering at home. I have been able to gradually piece that part of my life back together, but will never fully understand or recall that first month.

Every day since our accident has presented different challenges, all of which have to be met full-force. A few days after arriving at Craig, Robyn told me about what had happened with our accident and recounted the treatment that already occurred, and what was in the future, and told me about the outpouring of support not only in person, but also through phone calls and the Caring Bridge site. I then spent two days reading every journal entry, every guest book entry, every card and every email . . . many of which brought tears to my eyes. When I finally got home, I printed every one and will on occasion open them up and read them again—which still bring tears of gratitude . . . Everyone was so amazing!

In the time that I have had on Caring Bridge, I have not only written about my days and the therapy sessions, testing, X-rays and overall progress, but I have also shared some philosophical thoughts. I have always considered myself a devout Christian and supported the religious efforts of the faithful. I also believe that I consciously give extra consideration to those with special needs. My time at Craig only enhanced all those thoughts, and hopefully has made me a better person. The time there was extremely humbling in many ways. I have grown to appreciate everything and everyone around me—near or far. I had some pretty serious injuries, but through the grace of God, the treatment of professionals in their respective fields, and support from everyone, I have made it through the most difficult part of the journey. I however witnessed too many people who have not been so fortunate: persons with permanent physical disabilities, permanent mental disabilities, and some with both. But talk about the human spirit—these people "don't give up; they never give up," to quote former great North Carolina State basketball coach Jim Valvano.

That is something that we all need to remember in our lives—when we think things are difficult or relationships seem to be strained, we need to dig deep and find a solution to overcome these challenges . . . because I tell you, none of us have challenges that are so bad that we can't overcome them.

I would never wish on anyone the injuries that I have fought through and hope that all of you can appreciate the things that go on in our daily lives, because until you don't have those, you don't realize how special they are. I remember being able to drink my first glass of water, having that horrible feeding tube removed from my nose, taking that first bite of real food, walking to the bathroom by myself and getting to drive – all created a level of appreciation that you cannot attach an emotion to.

I have learned a tremendous amount about traumatic brain injuries, neck, skull and brain anatomy, and remember too many shocking facts: persons who suffer a TBI may fully recover in 2 years. But in those 2 years 20% of those injured, suffer a second injury—and the outcome of the second is not nearly as positive as the first.

In the immediate weeks following my discharge from Craig Hospital, I spent a lot of time by myself and thinking about how life has many ups, downs and detours, which are all unpredictable. In thinking about my own unpredictable routes, I realized that we learn so much from others and history . . . unfortunately, that education happens too often when someone is no longer available to directly learn from. A song gaining airplay immediately following my discharge was from a group called The Band Perry. They are a family band that released a song titled, *If I Die Young*. While I don't get excited about the title, I enjoy the melody and appreciate one specific verse.

"And maybe then you'll hear the words I been singin'
Funny when you're dead how people start listenin'"
I didn't die, and I believe that the words I have been saying have been heard. Don't look back and have regrets . . . look back and learn from every experience . . . but one experience you can never take for granted is being in this world with those you love.

Everyone I have had the pleasure of meeting has taught me something and I have learned a lot about myself and who I am through this entire event. At the end of the day, I look back and think about all the positive, and sometimes the not so positive things, and think about how I could or can make things better.

My time on earth is not done and I plan on taking advantage of every opportunity to be the best husband, son, brother, cousin, colleague and friend possible . . . you all have been the best for me.

THANK YOU!

Conclusion
_____

I WAS FINALLy released to work full-time in early January, and continued out-patient physical therapy thru September of 2012. Although I am not completely back to where I was prior to July 18, 2010, I am pretty close. I still experience stiffness in my neck, but have a range of motion far greater than what I would have if I had been treated by Halo or Fusion.

At the time of writing, I am still waiting for the FAA to grant me a 'Special Issuance' for my required medical certificate. Although I am not permitted to fly as Pilot in Command, I have still flown in the pilot's seat with an instructor. Things aren't as crisp as they were when I was flying regularly, but once I get that certificate back, I will jump back into the left seat and work on "polishing" those skills.

Brain injuries are an interesting challenge. No two TBI's are the same, and nobody responds exactly the same way from these injuries. I have been very fortunate with my injury, as I have full command of all my faculties; both my acuity and cognitive functions are good, and I only experience some residual effects . . . ones that only myself and those who truly know me will notice. A TBI is an injury that you never fully recover from . . . one you never want to experience, and certainly not a second one.

The challenges that both our families and I presented to the doctors and therapists resulted in great gains. Doctor Henderhiser took his knowledge and out of the box thinking to try a new technique known as 'Internal Stabilization,' which has allowed me to regain a neck function that would have normally been very limited had the standard model of care been followed.

The experience and knowledge gained from my barium swallow test and the end result have allowed other patients to skip the Upper GI tube and go straight to having their nasal feeding tubes removed so that they can eat sooner.

Just as I pushed hard to heal and recover, I will help push our kids to be successful as well. There are dreamers and there are doers . . . the only difference is that the dreamers make their dreams reality.

I spent almost six weeks at Craig Hospital, and our family made many special friends during our experience. Craig was a key resource for my recovery, and I believe that the Craig family made it possible for me to be a daddy – for that, I can never thank the Craig Family enough.

Since my experience, I have utilized as much time as possible promoting the Craig mission to advocate for patient needs and ways to support exemplary rehabilitation care to people affected by traumatic brain and spinal cord injuries so that they can achieve optimal health, independence, and life quality. Craig Hospital counts on patient and community support in order to provide opportunities for recovery to those who have suffered from a traumatic life changing moment.

The support we received during the recovering process from friends, family and colleagues was overwhelming and will never be truly expressed. There are so many people to thank:

- First – our families. Without you, the darkest days would have shed no light.
- Stephen for being such a great friend to us and being at my side at all times. For being the person Zedo and our families could rely on. You are a great part of our family.
- Kirschel and Sean for spreading the word, and being at the hospital when I got there, so I wasn't alone.
- Janet and Todd for all their support and creative thinking to find Zedo . . . for the continued support all through this time and for being such great friends.
- Damon for maintaining his commitment to us by providing emotional support throughout the entire hospital stay and flexibility while continuing the recovery. He never had a doubt that I would recover and come back strong as ever.
- Chris Martinez for his continued support – driving people wherever they needed to go, bringing food whenever he visited, for seeing us at every free moment.
- Wes for taking care of the house and helping with anything anyone needed.
- My friends and colleagues from CSC. All of your kind words, calls and emails . . . truly uplifting and appreciated. Additional thanks to Jay and Seyth for visiting while I was at my worst and giving Robyn support; and Seyth for returning in the fall to help

with "loose" ends around the house.
- Our good friend Scott for visiting us; for providing support and reading me the newspaper when I was still in my hospital bed and couldn't do anything for myself.
- The entire team at St Anthony's hospital . . . most of you I never met, but will always be grateful. Those of you who I did get to hug and shed a tear with: Jane, Sherry, Heather and Matt. You will always have a special place in our family.
- Dr. Henderhiser for thinking outside the box and taking a chance – it has paid off in ways that only we can understand

A special dedication to my wife. Robyn: you were the strongest person ever during this whole ordeal. You never lost hope and provided me with special motivation to push to be the best I could possibly be. The strength you have as a loving wife is truly remarkable, and I could have never asked for all that you gave. Every marriage and life faces challenges, but the ones we have already endured are a true testament of the love we get to share. I have been blessed to have you as a best friend and Mother of our children.

I love you!!!!

Craig is a special place! Don't wait until **you** need Craig, to discover how to redefine possible. To learn more about Craig Hospital, please go to: www.craighospital.org.

Proceeds from this book will be donated to the Craig Foundation to help support the mission of the hospital and their deeply committed and passionate staff.

Afterword

March 11, 2011 – 4:00 am

ROBYN SITS UP in bed and slides her legs to the side. I wake up and ask if she is okay.

"I think it's time," she says.

I help her out of bed, grab her clothes, then I get in the shower while she dresses. It could be a long day, so I have a bowl of cereal and we leave for the hospital.

We settle into our hospital room just after 8:00. Around 10:00, the Nurse asks Robyn to practice pushing, and she did . . . baby was starting to head out.

At 11:30, the Nurse and resident doctor have Robyn practice pushing again, but after only two practice pushes, the baby starts coming out and Robyn was told to stop until the doctor could get there.

The nurse calls for the doctor, who comes in to supervise the birth—and a few minutes later, bam!

"Congratulations! You have a little boy! Dad, do you want to cut the cord?"

I hold my son in my arms for the first time and say, "look . . . we have a little boy."

Robyn is tired, but holds out her hands. "Let me see..."

The nurse looks on with a smile on her face. Even though she must see this all the time, it has never gotten old. She asks, "Do you have a name picked out yet?"

"Yes we do . . . this is Matthew David"

April 18, 2013

PIPER, YOU ARE so different, but so much the same. We arrived at the hospital at 8:26 pm, and much like Matthew, your mom was told not to push. As time ticked by, the pace increased dramatically. When Robyn's water broke, she began strong contractions, and a nurse walking by our room, heard your mother in pain and came in. She saw that you were starting to head out, and she called for a Dr. Just like Matthew, 2 pushes and you were here . . . 11:26 pm – exactly 3 hours after arriving at the hospital.